My Family, KITTEN, & ME

Hands off My Pocket Money

D1471271

MARLÈNE PELMARD-LEVY

My Family, Kitten & Me Series

Book Two: Hands off My Pocket Money!

First published in the U.K. in 2023

Copyright © Marlène Pelmard-Levy

Unless authorised in writing, no part of this book may be reproduced or used in a manner inconsistent with the author's copyright. This prohibition applies to unauthorized uses or reproductions in any form, including electronic applications.

My Family, Kitten, & Me

Series

Book One - May I Introduce You to My Very Complicated Family?

Book Two - Hands off My Pocket Money!

Book Three - An Ever-Evolving Neighbourhood Web

Book Four - Can I Please Have a Crush Too?

Book Five - Could There Be a Thread of Truth in Fake News?

Book Six - Down but Not Out

Check out **My Family, Kitten, & Me Series** on my Facebook, Twitter and Instagram.

DEDICATION

When I was a child, I knew either one or both of my parents would always be home to welcome me back from school every day.

Years later, when I went to study in Martinique, often I would want to hear their voices or share some news with them, and I knew one of them would always pick up the phone.

Though England has been my home for many years now, in some ways, it feels as if I never left my native country, Guadeloupe, because the bond that has been nurtured from the day I was born has transcended time and distance.

From time to time, Mum would remind me that life is not a fairy tale and that someday I would receive a phone call with some sad news. She was right. Sickness, accident, and death have extended their brutal hand on too many of those so dear to me, including my most loving and caring parents. It is in their memory that I wrote this series composed of factual as well as fictitious stories.

Marlène

For many years now, my parents have introduced a budget that is applied to the pocket money we receive. We give ten per cent to a cause that is dear to our hearts, we keep twenty per cent for our personal expenses, and we save seventy per cent. I must emphasise that I use part of my pocket money to buy presents for my parents when it is their birthday or anniversary, I also buy birthday presents for my siblings, and I always carry in my purse at least two fifty pence coins in case I meet a homeless person. Besides, my siblings and I sponsor three children in a developing country. It may not sound like a lot to you, but it is a lot to me.

CONTENTS

CHAPTER ONE

A LIFE-CHANGING TRIP

Last year, my parents opened a mini current account for Brigitte on her thirteenth birthday. She has her own debit card, so she can withdraw money from any cashpoint and even use her card to pay for her own shopping, whether in a physical retail shop or an online store.

Next year, they will open one for Ravel, Luke, and Chelsea. I'm sure you're wondering when it will be my turn. Well, I don't want to disappoint you, but the truth is, I am at the tail-end of the queue. I must wait another five long years unless the government changes the law. Doesn't that make you sick?

I can't blame my parents for giving birth to me five years after Brigitte since they were young then, and they had probably not thought of which birth order would be in my best interest. Since I will have to live with this big age gap between us for the rest of my life, I have decided to accept it as gracefully as I can. But if you don't mind me saying, just between you and me, I have suffered a great deal as a result of my parents' lack of foresight.

Ever since they have given Brigitte a debit card, I have wrestled with this issue in my head countless times and analysed it from every possible angle. It boils down to one thing: age privilege. Now let's be fair! There isn't that much difference between an eight-year-old and a thirteen-year-old. I can count, I can write, and I can even analyse complex numbers. There are many things that thirteen-year-olds don't know and cannot do. Although Brigitte is good at Maths, she still uses a calculator for difficult computation.

I understand that banks want to make sure we do not make a payment when there are no funds in our accounts. But adults overspend all the time. I heard it on the news again earlier this week. If the banks are worried about their reputation or going bankrupt, all they need to do is have a written agreement between us and them. I am more than willing to promise not to overspend, and if I ever do, accidentally of course, they can recover their money from Mummy or Daddy's joint bank account.

Brigitte said the bank wants children—actually, she didn't say children—she said the bank wants young people to learn how to manage money and become more responsible investors and spenders. When I thought about it, it occurred to me that our system is flawed. The banks are indirectly suggesting it is OK to be irresponsible and that children don't need to learn to manage money until they reach thirteen. Does that make sense to you?

As I see it, I have two options. I can spend all my pocket money on my whims and fancies, chalking it up to my lack of maturity, or I can come up with a strong financial plan that will include careful spending, savings, and investing, thus proving to the bank that children as young as eight are financially literate. Though the first option is really tempting, I'd rather think long term as always.

I haven't researched this, but I believe one of the main reasons a lot of adults still cannot manage money is because their parents didn't teach them when they were my age. I most certainly don't want to end up like them. I want to prove that eight-year-olds can manage money and can be responsible if they are taught and given the chance. I haven't told my parents about my projects yet, and I don't want to say too much to you either at this point, just in case. I'll just share the basics with you if you don't mind.

It all started when we went to Paris for a week, at the end of term earlier this year. As we were about to board the aircraft, a stand full of magazines and newspapers on the left side of the passenger boarding bridge caught my eye. They were all free and there for anyone regardless of their age. I was thrilled. This was my chance to further educate myself on money management and finances. I freed myself from Daddy's hand and went to help myself. I asked Daddy which ones had a few pages on finances. He was surprised at my question.

"Did you say finances?"

"Yes, Daddy, I mean the pages about finances and also the economy."

"Right, right," he uttered while helping me search the relevant ones. He looked a bit nervous and awkward. I think he realised I had outgrown the basic teachings he and Mum had taught me about money. I chose three different newspapers and two magazines, including one in French.

As soon as the two air hostesses welcomed us onboard and directed us to our seats, I asked Grande Loulou not to sit next to me as I would need lots of space when I opened my newspapers to read them. She was not amused. I discreetly reminded her we were in a public space, and she needed to carry herself with dignity, just like I did. She just walked away and sat next to Mummy.

"Honey, let me fasten your seat," Daddy offered.

"Thank you, Daddy, but I can manage all by myself," I replied.

"Are you going to read all these newspapers and magazines on the flight?"

"Oh, yes. I have a lot of catching up to do."

"I see." He looked intrigued; however, I'm sure he was proud to have such a sensible daughter. But I had a problem. A big one. The newspaper was so big and had so many pages that I found it hard to turn the pages over. It was the same one delivered to our porch every day, but it looked so much bigger on the plane. I bent over to Daddy and whispered in his ears, "Daddy, could you please help me turn the pages over without making it obvious? I want the pages about finances, stock and shares, things like that."

He glanced at me and returned a complicit smile. "Well, let's find out what's going on in the world of finance, shall we?" he suggested.

Luke and Ravel looked in our direction and shook their heads.

"Looking at these numbers and these ..." I couldn't remember what those pictures were called. I looked around me, then discreetly bent toward Daddy and whispered, "What are these called again?"

"They are graphs. G-R-A-P-H-S," he whispered back to me.

I started again. "Looking at these numbers and these graphs, it seems a lot has been happening; wouldn't you say so, Daddy?" I said it loud enough so the members of my family could hear.

"I have to agree, honey."

"Daddy, could you please comment on those different parts so I can understand them? Do it in a way that shows I know what you're talking about," I whispered again.

"Sure." Daddy pointed at the section we were looking at.

"The pound is down again," he said with a concerned voice. "That's not good for our economy."

"Down again! That's too bad. Not good at all for our economy," I commented.

"The value of the dollar has been steadily declining too. Well, it looks as if gas and oil prices will be on the rise again."

"It seems inevitable, doesn't it, Daddy? That's not good news at all. I feel sorry for all the families who will not be able to afford to pay their gas and electricity bill. Sometimes I wonder if those in charge really know what they are doing and if they care about people."

We silently read and turned the pages over. Daddy pointed to a paragraph on the left.

"This business has been operating for about two centuries. It's sad that it may go into liquidation. Because of poor management, thousands of people will lose their jobs."

"I could see it coming. They should have done something about the situation years ago. It's a pity that so many people will now lose their jobs, isn't it?" I responded.

"It's deeply upsetting."

"Do you think the government might take some action to save the company?" I continued.

"Quite possibly. Yes. Quite possibly."

"I think the government should, and the directors should give an account to the taxpayers; don't you think?"

"I completely agree with you, honey."

"Our economy is in such a mess. I don't know how the government is going to fix it. It gets more complicated every day. Well, let's hope for the best," I sighed loudly while shaking my head.

"You're right. We can only hope for the best."

I continued reading and glanced at Daddy from time to time. I feigned not to see or hear Mum and my siblings talking about me.

"I'm so relieved these two companies have merged. It will save thousands of jobs and give a boost to the economy. But do you know what I'm even happier about?"

Daddy looked at me with inquisitive eyes.

"I am extremely happy when companies don't move their head offices abroad to save money or to avoid paying taxes. I do understand they want to make a big profit, but they must also think of what is best for our country. They can't leave it to people like you and me to pay all the taxes and on top of that find jobs for all the unemployed."

"You are very insightful."

"I think the government needs to come up with a much stronger plan so that businesses will never want to move abroad."

"What should the government do, in your opinion?" Daddy asked.

"They can make them pay taxes but not too much. We wouldn't want them to get discouraged. What's that word again? In…incen…"

"Incentives," Daddy said.

"That's it. Give them some good incentives. I don't mean peanuts. Reward them when they are good to their employees and their customers. And give them a big reward if they allow parents to work from home so they can spend more time with their children and their elderly parents, especially if they are sick. Do you know that many older people would love that?"

"Definitely. You're spot on."

"Daddy, things are moving so fast in the financial world. If I'm not careful, I can easily fall behind."

"You're right about that. I completely agree."

"Do you find that you can't keep up at times?"

"I certainly do."

"Same here. Do you know that I hadn't given much thought to Forex trading because I thought it was like gambling? I only recently realised that it is not the case. I started learning about it so that by the time I turn 18, I'll be ready to do online trading. And Daddy, do you know what else I found out the other day?"

"What did you find out?"

"Well, I found out that AI is going to play a major role in the financial world. So, it is crucially important that you and mummy keep up with this new technology so that our financial education does not suffer. Think about it. If we don't keep up with this new technology, we won't be able to help children around the world."

"We will do our best to keep up with all those new developments, so you and your siblings get good value for money, sweetheart."

"Oh, that's great!"

We both smiled.

The passenger in the other row was also reading a financial newspaper. I could tell he was in awe. He glanced in our direction a few times as Daddy and I were talking business. I nodded in acknowledgement of our common interest. He responded by nodding his head too. When he could no longer contain himself, he put aside his newspapers, turned toward Daddy and me, and said quite loudly, "Clever little girl you've got there. It's not every day you see a child with such a keen interest in finance and the economy."

"Oh, she is very clever," Daddy replied, glancing at me with a faint smile.

"How old is she? You don't mind me asking?"

"She is eight."

"Eight? Wow! I am amazed. Nowadays, children are hooked on social media, video games, celebrities, and whatnot. She is an exception. She will go far. I have eight- and fifteen-year-old daughters. They show no interest in finance or anything that happens in the country. They are addicted to their mobile phones. It's a fight to get them to put them down. You are fortunate to have a daughter who, at this age, has such a keen interest in finance and the economy. Very fortunate. In a few years, she might become the governor of the Bank of England, or the Chancellor of the Exchequer. You never know. I don't think we have ever had a woman in those offices. She might be the first. It will be a nice change." Then he fixed his eyes on me and added, "Keep it up, young lady; you will go far in life."

I tried to contain my excitement. I didn't want him to think I was not familiar with the things he had just said, or I had not thought of them before. I nodded my head and said out of courtesy, "Thank you, sir. That is so very kind of you."

Another passenger had been listening to our conversation. She asked the other passenger who was talking to us if she had heard correctly that I was only eight years old. She was astonished. She got out of her seat, walked to our row, and stood in the corridor.

"I must apologise for the intrusion, but I had to get out of my seat to see with my own eyes who was this eight-year-old girl reasoning like a well-informed adult."

Daddy and I glanced at each other. For the first time in my life, I realised I had some influence, and I could be taken seriously.

"What a precious daughter you have! Simply amazing!" she continued.

"Oh, thank you," Daddy responded.

"What would you like to be when you grow up?" she asked.

Before I had time to answer, she realised she had failed to follow protocol. She quickly said, "Oh, pardon me! My name is Grace. I am delighted to meet you."

"I'm Petite Loulou. I am very pleased to meet you too."

We talked like two adults. I was, however, glad when the air hostess came around and joined in the conversation. I was a bit afraid to be out of my depth. Mum and my siblings had been watching the conversation all along. They all winked at me and gave me a thumbs-up.

The conversation didn't stop when Grace and the air hostess left. We could hear them talking about me with other passengers.

"It's nice to be the centre of attention once in a while. The only thing is you don't want people to ask you questions you don't know the answers to. It can make you look silly, isn't that so Daddy?"

"I doubt there will be a question you won't find an answer to," he said with a big grin on his face. "But in the event that you cannot find an answer, remember that none of us knows everything. It takes a great deal of maturity to admit that we do not know everything." He reached out to hug me, planted a giant kiss on my forehead, and combed my hair with the palm of his hand.

"What would my world be without my little sunshine?" he added.

I put my arms around his neck and gave him a big kiss. Mum and my siblings were dying to find out what we were talking and giggling about. They made all sorts of gestures with their mouths, heads, and hands to get us to include them. With my hands, I gestured that the conversation was between

Daddy and me, and the empty seat next to me was not empty as such. I needed it to rest my newspapers and magazines.

Soon it was snack time. The strong smell of tea and coffee prevailed over the aroma of orange and apple juices. The air hostess gave me an extra snack and said a good working brain needed an extra supply of healthy food. That was very kind of her. I'm sure she would have offered me a seat in first class if I were on my own. She must have thought she couldn't leave out Daddy and the rest of my family. That would have been very unprofessional. Next time we travel abroad, I will sit on my own. I know my parents will not like the idea, but as a compromise, they can sit in a row close by.

"Daddy, what does the Governor of England and the charity something do?" I discreetly asked when nobody was around.

He didn't understand my question. I leaned toward him and reminded him the passenger across said I might be the first woman to occupy these positions.

"Oh, I see. You mean the Governor of the Bank of England and the Chancellor of the Exchequer?"

"Yes, that's it. Could you please write it down for me?" I asked very quietly.

Daddy wrote it down and did quite a good job at explaining each of them. I thought about what the passengers said about me and those positions. These are extremely important positions. Maybe one day I could really become the governor of the Bank of England or the Chancellor of the Exchequer. I had always thought being the Prime Minister was the best job. This conversation was definitely an eye-opener.

"I need your advice. I don't know which one to choose out of the three."

"Honey, you don't need to choose now. It's always good to keep an open mind. When we get to France, or back home, we can do some research so that you become more familiar with what those positions entail."

"OK, Daddy. But which one pays more?"

"I think the governor of the Bank of England has the highest salary, but you also want to take into consideration the perks. It's spelled P-E-R-K-S."

"What are perks?"

"They are some extra advantages you get because of your job. It can be something like a mobile phone, a company car, or a house, for instance."

"Daddy, how come you didn't tell me about perks before? You only told me about bonuses. Do you get a salary and perks too?"

"Yes, I do. My car is a company car. Plus, I get free holidays for the family and private healthcare."

"I didn't know that's how it works. You mean I can have both a good salary and the perks?

"Most definitely, that is, if you choose a job that offers some perks besides your salary."

"Will I have to pay taxes?"

"I'm afraid you will have to."

"I don't mind paying taxes as long as it is no more than what I get for my pocket money. Do you give away a lot of your money to the government?"

"More than I want."

"Can't you think of something you can do with your money, so you don't give so much to the government?" I felt outraged.

"I wish it was that simple. Honey, I don't give it away. The government takes it."

"But why do you let them take it? Why don't you tell them you need it to open another bank account for all your children so they have money to pay for their university fees or so that each one will be able to buy a house? You always say you want to do more for the homeless children and adults. You could tell the government you need the money to help them. I'm sure if you have a good plan and explain it to them, they will let you keep the money."

"Hmm."

"Ravel has been reading some of your books on money. He told me that rich people don't pay taxes. If you pay taxes, that means you are poor. Daddy, are you poor?"

"If, according to your definition, paying taxes means you are poor, well, your daddy is poor, but I am working on improving my financial situation."

"I really hope you won't take too long. If you don't hurry, you will die poor and you will feel sorry that you gave all your money to the government instead of your children."

"Honey don't worry. We will be OK."

"There is no way I'm going to let the government take my money. I'm going to decide how much I give them."

"Good for you! Do you realise there is a lot of wisdom in what you've just said?"

"Of course, Daddy. I've been thinking about it for a very long time now."

We had some of our snacks, and I shared some of mine with Grande Loulou, who was seated in the other aisle.

"So, do you have an idea of which of these three jobs might interest you the most?"

"I don't think it will be difficult for me to choose."

"No?"

"Not at all. I am a hundred per cent sure I will choose the one that has the highest salary and all the perks. I would like a job that gives me lots of holidays, lots of perks, a car, and a house."

"Well, I believe you will make the right choice. You may also want to set up your own business. In that case you will be your own boss and have the luxury to decide how you want to manage your time and your money."

"Mummy told me that having multiple sources of income is the best way toward financial independence."

"Mummy is right. She knows what she is talking about. You can take a leaf from her book."

"I've already done so, Daddy."

"Good on you. I know you can reach the top."

"Don't worry, Daddy. When I reach the top, I will help you reach the top too. I will also help my siblings and even Mummy."

"Oh, thank you. It's so comforting to know you won't leave Daddy at the bottom of the ladder."

"Oh, no. I will make sure you reach the top too."

"Thank you. That is very generous of you."

"You're welcome. Daddy, do you think I will be able to help all the children who are poor in the world if I am rich?"

"It will depend on how rich you are."

"I would like to have enough money so that not a single child lives in poverty."

"That is a noble ambition. Helping those in need is what life is all about. Keep that spirit, baby; don't ever lose sight of what truly matters."

"Thanks, Daddy. One of these days, I'm going to go with Mummy to one of her conferences that educates people about money. Would you like to come with me?"

"Oh, yes, I would love to. I can't turn down such an offer, especially when it comes from my own daughter," he replied with a witty smile.

"Oh, good. I will let you know when the next conference is taking place. I'll find out from Mummy."

"Thanks, sweetheart. I'm so grateful."

"You're welcome."

I picked the aircraft magazine in front of my seat and browsed through the first few pages. Daddy continued to read the newspaper. After a short pause we resumed our conversation.

"Daddy, I wonder what other important things you haven't told me about that can have a big impact on my life. "

He stared at me, looking very surprise. I placed both my hands on each side of his cheeks to prevent his head from moving.

"Look at me straight in the eyes and tell me you are still my daddy."

"Honey, of course I am your daddy and will always be."

"Now promise me you will teach me everything you know about how I can make money and how I can invest in stocks and shares and become rich. I really need to help other children around the world; this is an urgent matter."

"But honey, don't you realise that's what Mummy and I have been doing?"

"Yes, but at this crucial stage of my life, I need to step up."

"Got you. We will step up."

"Do you promise?"

"I promise, sunshine."

"If I had my business card, I would have given one to Grace, one to the air hostess, and one to the other passengers. I really hate to lose out on those opportunities," I mumbled.

He gave me a broad smile and nodded. I was about to glance through another magazine when a thought came to my mind.

"Do you think I should wear more mature clothes like a suit and buy darker-coloured handbags?"

"Why, sweetheart?"

"Because businesswomen wear only dark-coloured suits."

"Who wears dark-coloured suits?"

Unexpectedly, Grande Loulou joined in the conversation without being invited. I was stunned. I had to say something.

"Grande Loulou, don't you know it's rude to eavesdrop on people's conversations and interrupt? It is very unprofessional, and besides it is not ladylike."

Although she is older than I am, sometimes she doesn't act her age. I spend a great deal of time correcting her mistakes and teaching her about life.

"Daddy, can I please come and sit next to you? Now it's my turn," Grande Loulou said. She made it sound as if sitting next to Daddy was a matter of life and death.

"Grande Loulou, I wanted to speak with Daddy about some personal matters, and now you want to spoil everything. That is so selfish. Mummy must feel so sad because you have abandoned her."

"I just want to spend a bit of time with Daddy too. That's all," she argued.

"Well, I think Grande Loulou can join us. Daddy has to share his time with his other children too," he said while glancing at me.

I was not happy. Bad timing. Really bad timing. "Grande Loulou didn't even book this slot," I moaned.

"What slot are you talking about? Daddy is my daddy too, you know. I don't need to book a slot to spend time with him. Petite Loulou, stop being bossy."

"Honey, I understand you wanted us to continue this conversation, and we will. But let's make room for Grande Loulou. If you were in her shoes, you would want her to make room for you, wouldn't you?"

Grande Loulou knew that Daddy was on her side. She moved closer to my seat and showcased her victory with a triumphant grin on her face. I reluctantly nodded and slowly moved my newspapers and magazines.

"I will sit in the middle so both of you can have a bit of Daddy, all right?"

Daddy and I got up so that Grande Loulou could sit near the window. I must confess that at first, I tried to make it hard for her to participate in the conversation. But once I adjusted to her being with us, I enjoyed listening to her tell us about the new book she was reading. We played board games together until the plane was about to land in Paris.

I love France. It's home too. We dropped off our luggage in our bedrooms and ran to give our neighbours some goodies from good old England and to catch up with the latest news. As always, they had saved some goodies for us too and took us on a tour around their farm, showing us all the new things they had acquired. Their pets warmly welcomed us back. *C'est beau la vie. Vive la France.*

CHAPTER TWO

◆◆◇◆◆

KITTEN AND HER VERY SUSPICIOUS BOYFRIEND

When we were getting ready to go to bed, Daddy's phone rang. It was Grandad facetiming Daddy. It was about Kitten. We had left her with our grandparents. There was a mini crisis on the other side of the English Channel. I'm so used to crises in our family.

"Robert, we offered Kitten half the cheese, but she refused to eat it," Grandad said. He was very concerned; so was Grandma.

"At first, we thought she didn't want it, so we put it back in the fridge. She has been complaining ever since. Your dad went back to the fridge to get it and offer it to her once again, but she still wouldn't touch it. She doesn't want us to put it away, but she won't eat it either. We don't know what to do," Grandma added.

"Hmm, she won't eat it? Kitten has never refused to eat her cheese. She will not sleep without having it," Daddy commented.

"Not that cheese is good for her health in the first place," Grandma added.

"Try telling her that," Dad replied. "Do you think we haven't told her a zillion times? Kitten loves her cheese. Besides, Petite Loulou told us that since Kitten is French, eating cheese will not negatively affect her health.

Grandma and Grandad cracked up with laughter. "Our apology, Kitten. Indeed, *tu es aussi française*," Grandad said.

"Meow, meow."

"She is not sick or has some discomfort, has she?"

"No, I don't think so. She has been playing with us."

"Where is she?" asked Dad.

Grandad adjusted his phone so we could see Kitten.

"I can see her now."

When Kitten saw Dad, she meowed even louder.

"What's the matter, baby cat?"

Kitten kept meowing. She was complaining, but she didn't make clear what she was complaining about.

"Mum, where did you put the cheese?"

"Well, in her plate, of course. We washed it first, placed it on her mat, and placed half the cheese on it."

"Ah, that's why she didn't eat it. You need to place it in the palm of your hand. That's how she eats it. You need to sit on your bed so she can sit next to you. I thought we had told you."

"Did you hear that, Allan?" Grandma asked Grandad.

"What did he say we should do?" he asked while walking toward the fridge.

"Bring back the cheese, Allan. We need to sit on our bed and place the cheese in the palm of our hand. That's how she eats it."

"Goodness gracious! Robert, don't you think you spoil Kitten too much? I've never seen a cat so fussy. She only eats food that is on her plate, which must be on her special mat. You need to put her own sheet on the bed for her to sleep on. And now we need to sit on the bed and place the cheese in the palm of our hand, or she won't eat it. Goodness gracious!"

"Let me see if she will eat it now. Come, Kitten."

Kitten jumped on the bed next to Grandma. Grandma placed the cheese in the palm of her hand under the watchful eye of Kitten. She glanced at Grandma, meowed, and started eating.

Grandma and Grandad burst out laughing. "It would be useful to write an instruction manual to make sure Kitten is comfortable when she spends her holiday with us," she suggested.

I'm telling you Kitten is fussy. Very fussy. We had to facetime her every day and sound unenthusiastic about our holiday. We had to keep telling her she was so fortunate to spend her holiday with Grandma and Grandad. Otherwise, we might have ended up with a mini revolution. That would have been too much for our grandparents to handle.

When we returned from our holiday, for six or seven consecutive days, Kitten disappeared in the morning and came back for lunch. She disappeared again until late afternoon. Nobody knew where she went, not even Daddy.

One day, when she came back for lunch, she was accompanied by another cat. Ravel was the first one to make his acquaintance. He called Daddy and told him that Kitten wanted to introduce her new boyfriend to him. None of us knew Kitten had a boyfriend, but we thought she was very courteous in asking him to wait outside.

"Ravel, how do you know it's her boyfriend?" Daddy asked.

"I assume so."

"For all we know, this cat might be just a friend," Daddy commented.

When we went outside, we met this new cat. He looked fairly decent. It didn't take Daddy long to work out the reason for Kitten's daily disappearance. Kitten was getting to know her new acquaintance before taking him home. Daddy talked to Kitten, then to Kitten's guest.

I don't think he is ready to see Kitten with a boyfriend. He thinks she is still a baby cat. Whatever his feelings were, Daddy managed the situation quite well, especially since Kitten didn't give him any notice or warning. He invited the cat inside and placed a plate on the floor for him next to Kitten's plate. As soon as Chelsea put some food on the plate for him, he devoured it. Bits of food fell off the plate. He searched for them and ate every bit. Then he licked the surface of the floor where he had eaten the bits of food.

From time to time, Kitten would raise her head to observe him. I don't think she was impressed by his lack of good manners. He even asked for seconds, so Chelsea gave him some more.

When he finished eating his seconds, he took a step or two toward Kitten's plate to help himself. Kitten didn't like that and stopped him. Poor Kitten, she must have felt so embarrassed by his behaviour, especially in our presence. When they finished eating, they both disappeared.

He returned the following day, and the next, for lunch. He behaved the same way every single time.

Halfway through the week, early in the morning, we heard a cat purring outside. Suddenly, Kitten's ears stood up straight and forward. She listened for a moment, jumped off the chair, and disappeared through the cat flap. Grande Loulou and I spied on her through the glass door. It was her boyfriend. He came to tell her something, and they both left.

They would leave in the morning and return for lunch every day. We would occasionally glance at them during the afternoon; they would disappear at some point; and she would return home, on her own, around six o'clock in the evening. Ravel, Brigitte, Luke, and Chelsea said that Kitten and her boyfriend were going steady, and we should prepare ourselves for a happy event any day now.

Caleb said that Kitten will have to teach her new boyfriend table manners, but otherwise, he seemed like quite a good cat. Caleb thought the new cat was good company for Kitten. I didn't quite agree. I told Caleb and Grande Loulou he might be an impostor and take advantage of Kitten.

About three weeks later, Kitten spent the whole day with us. Her boyfriend didn't come home. We wondered what had happened, but Kitten was silent on the matter. We never saw this so-called boyfriend again. So, we concluded they had split up. Kitten must have realised he wasn't a good deal after all.

She didn't seem sad, lovesick, or anything like that, though. She ate and behaved as normal, unless, of course, she was trying hard to hide her true feelings so we wouldn't worry about her.

A few days later, Grande Loulou and I saw the cat at one of our neighbours' houses, playing with their cat in the garden. We had been wondering all along if he had died or if he had been sick.

I told Grande Loulou I was right. I knew all along he was an impostor, and we'd better tell our friends so they could warn Missy, their cat. Otherwise he could easily break her heart. We didn't see eye to eye. She thought the cat might be just a friend, and we didn't even know if the cat was a he or a she.

When we got home, I told Ravel, Brigitte, Luke, and Chelsea about Kitten and her boyfriend's affair. They all thought Kitten must have put an end to the relationship because he was not quite up to her standard. That made me feel better. I wouldn't want Kitten to be cheated on and fall into depression. I thought it best not to mention it to her as it's never wise to stir up painful memories. Let her heal in peace.

CHAPTER THREE

PROJECTS ON THE MOVE

Since my celebrity moment on the flight to Paris, the whole clan has been determined to take their financial education to the next level. I can't blame them. I suppose it doesn't look good on them if I steal the show all the time. My brothers and sisters have thoroughly searched our parents' bookcases and identified a fine collection of seventeen books on money.

Because of this additional pursuit, Brigitte had to review our morning schedule. Instead of getting up at six-thirty on our school days, we all agreed to wake up half an hour earlier so we could devote some time to working on our individual projects. I never complained even once about getting up a whole half an hour earlier. I surprised myself.

Our parents were completely oblivious to our new plans and schedule. We wanted to do some reading and come up with a clear plan before telling them about our projects. Ravel suggested the boys work together on their goals in their bedroom while the girls worked in Brigitte and Chelsea's bedroom to avoid any suspicion from our parents.

The self-appointed boss assigned each of us a book she expected us to finish reading before the end of the week. She gave Grande Loulou and I small books to read. I'm sure you have read between the lines. If it had not been for Grande Loulou, she would have given me a much thicker book, but, of course, she didn't want to cause our sister any embarrassment. That was wise of her.

She also invited Grande Loulou to join us in our morning meeting. Look, Brigitte knows very well that Grande Loulou is more of a liability than an asset, but we couldn't leave her out. I'm sure she will pick up one or two things along the way. And when it gets too technical, I will make myself available to break it down for her. After all, that's what sisters are for.

We spent the first two weeks reading our books and taking notes. We had a short meeting every morning. Brigitte had scheduled a business meeting the following Monday, during our school break, while our parents were preparing breakfast. It was a real business meeting chaired by her and Ravel. Chelsea and Luke were the secretaries. We shared what we had learned from our readings, and the chairs told the secretaries what to write on the big flipchart. It was quite intense, especially for Grande Loulou. I instinctively knew when she felt completely lost, and I would systematically ask the chair to clarify some concepts for the benefit of all of us.

At the end of those couple of weeks, we had a more thorough knowledge of how to generate and invest money. In fact, we learned a great deal about the financial market in general. Each of us now had a clear project. Ravel and Brigitte were satisfied that our individual plans were both comprehensive and realistic. I felt ready to play a crucial role in the financial markets.

All in all, our first business meeting was a complete success. It was both productive and orderly. I feel our next one should be recorded so we can send a videoclip to the Speaker of the House of Commons because it pains me to see our MPs, who are supposed to be grown-ups, throwing so many tantrums when they are supposed to be working for the country and the people. I often wonder what other countries think of us when they watch our sittings.

On the Saturday evening, Caleb and Grande Loulou asked Mum and Dad if they could help them with their projects the following morning after breakfast. They had no idea what we had in mind.

As soon as we awoke the following day, Ravel and Brigitte gave us our assignments. Caleb was to ensure that Mum and Dad stayed in the kitchen to prepare breakfast, Chelsea and Luke were to move some of the furniture around the study, Ravel and Brigitte were to put up our notes on the wall, and Grande Loulou and I were to help them. Kitten was not assigned any specific task. Only professionals could deal with such an operation. I had one more assignment: to suggest we have breakfast on the patio, and the others would back me up. That was our strategy to keep our parents far from the study.

We got up early on the Sunday morning and had a short business meeting in the study. Everything was ready for the big reveal. We tried very hard to hide our excitement.

"Caleb and Grande Loulou are you ready for your homework?" asked Mummy not long after breakfast.

"Yes, we are. We've already put our work in the study. We'll join you and Daddy as soon as we've brushed our teeth," Grande Loulou responded.

The spies were lying in wait, monitoring their parents. You've pulled some strings. You have all the pieces of the puzzle together, and now you're just lying in wait, knowing it's just a matter of seconds.

If you've never planned a surprise for your parents and spied on them to see their reaction, you should try it. I can't tell you how great it feels to know you have outsmarted your own parents. You can feel your heart racing. You can feel the electricity racing through arms and legs to your fingers and toes. You find yourself sniffing, almost like dogs and cats, in search for clues and pricking up your ears, desperate for more evidence. You've been handed a script to play the part of a private detective, and you know the case is about to be solved. It feels heroic.

Once we were sure they had taken the bait and they were exactly where we wanted them, we knew their excited curiosity would get the better of them and their senses would not be satisfied until they had fully inspected the mysterious writing on the wall. We came out of our hiding place and marched toward them.

As soon as they turned their heads in our direction, we knew our plan had worked. A deep sense of pride - the proper kind of pride, of course - and a thousand hugs and kisses filled the air. Our parents were thrilled. They were too moved to say much at first. They also realised their children were more intelligent than they had given them credit for. They wanted to know every detail about our project. Nothing gave me more satisfaction than hearing them ask how we had come up with such a brilliant idea and hearing my siblings unanimously respond it was thanks to me. Their answer gave me goosebumps.

I often talked to Kitten about this key moment in my life. I suppose by now, she must be familiar with Neil Armstrong's name because I've told her at least a dozen times that what I experienced on that day must have been like what Neil Armstrong experienced when he walked on the moon in 1969.

You and I know all too well that it's not easy to be self-motivated and to work as a team and define a clear project, especially one as technical as ours. No adults could achieve what we achieved over a couple of weeks, unless, of course, they had attended a motivational seminar and were familiar with the world of finance.

Ravel is very insightful. I can always count on him to handle tricky situations. He was truly the best person to let our parents know they needn't feel bad if they didn't understand everything about finance and investments because there were many other ways they could lend their support. They enthusiastically offered to do so. That was exactly what we wanted to hear. They didn't have a clue about the kind of support we were expecting from them. Next time, we will get them to confirm their commitment to support us. I asked Chelsea to get it recorded; then they won't be able to pull out. Our final step will be to send them our invoice.

We have since made a lot more progress. I dare say that Grande Loulou has been doing pretty well. I made a commitment to coach her from the beginning so she can be on par with the rest of us.

Did you just ask if she is feeling a bit frustrated because she is not able to process all the information? Well, not at all. If anything, I think she believes she might be even more clever than the rest of us. Mind you, she understands a lot of complex concepts. In fact, she gets a hundred per cent of them right, even before I get a chance to work them out in my own head, and she asks very clever questions. Sounds fishy to you too, right? I think one of our older siblings fills her in about the topic for discussion well in advance, or she gets private tutoring from one of them. I will most definitely carry out my own investigation and keep you updated. But thanks for the tip.

If you come to our house, you will see a giant planner on Ravel, Caleb, and Luke's bedroom wall. It is divided into three big columns and ten rows. Each of them has written his name and his individual goals. They have worked out what they want to achieve in the short- and long-term and the steps they need to take at each stage to reach their goals. They hold each other accountable and compete among themselves to be the first to reach their goal. They also race to be ahead of us. It's true that boys are usually more competitive than girls.

Brigitte and Chelsea have decided to have their own personal planner. So, Grande Loulou and I decided to do the same. We have all pinned our planners on the wall on top of our desk. You should see Brigitte's planner. I have never seen anything like it. From the big boss' viewpoint, every single day must be a highly productive day. I fear the day she becomes manager of her own company, because not only will she be working around the clock, but everything within the walls of her company will be following the same rhythm. I don't mean she will treat her employees like slaves. She has a good heart and stands against any form of abuse. But trust me, she will program all the equipment in her company to continue to work long after her employees have left, six days a week, whether it be night or bank holidays. I told her she will need a highly sophisticated remote-control system for her office equipment and several cameras to ensure all her machines are working to maximum capacity, and that none sit idle. She will also have to take out extra insurance to cover those machines as she should expect regular mechanical breakdowns. She just laughed it off.

I wish I could tell you more about our projects but judging from all the details my siblings have written on their planner, there is no way they would allow me to put them in the public domain. Sharing copyrighted material with you might get me into serious trouble and tarnish my reputation for ever. If I were six or seven years old, I might get away with it, but I am eight now, so the law might not be so lenient.

I was, however, considering sharing the details of my projects with you as I have no doubt you could truly benefit from them. They might even inspire you to start your own project. In the end, however, I thought it wiser not to. I wouldn't want you to think I am boasting or deduce there is no way my siblings' work could compare with mine. But if you really insist on finding out about my personal contribution, don't hesitate to drop me a line. I will be more than happy to email a summary to you so you can share it with your family and friends with my compliments. I only request that you visit my social media platforms and add a nice comment. Not only will it improve my ratings, but it will also place me in a most favourable position to produce more copyrighted videos and other materials.

CHAPTER FOUR

POCKET MONEY CRISIS

Three days ago I went through my notes to ensure I had included everything in my financial project. Fortunately I only had to elaborate on a couple of points. I was very pleased with my progress.

This reminds me that I didn't tell you we regularly listen to seminars and podcasts about finances, motivational speaking, and goal setting.

Yesterday I listened to a seminar by Mr. Sterling, my favourite financial expert. He has a live radio show each week, and the topic this week was "pocket money." I thought it was high time he dealt with this topic because I was due for a pay rise, and my parents had not made any mention of it. I was looking forward to emailing them the link so that once they had listened to his show, they would take some practical steps toward redeeming themselves.

Once Mr. Sterling had answered a couple of questions from his listeners who had some specific financial concerns, he introduced the topic. I had my notepad ready to write every point that was applicable to my case.

"If you have just joined us, today's topic is about pocket money. I know some of you don't want to hear this but listen to me. We are raising a lazy generation that doesn't want to work and expects their parents to give them regular pocket money. Their parents buy them food, which they eat free of charge at least three times a day, and they insist on wearing the latest designer clothes and trainers. Their mamas do their laundry, iron their clothes, and even tidy up their bedrooms. And these children expect their parents to give them enough pocket money so they can take their girlfriends or boyfriends to restaurants, concerts, and what have you. They do not make any positive contributions to the household. All they do is take, take, and take," Mr. Sterling stated.

I could feel the tension rising in my body. Was he talking about me? The pen I was going to take notes with fell from my hand, and I couldn't pick it up, though I tried.

"Parents, if this is the scenario in your home, you have to put a stop to it. You must stop giving your big children pocket money that they spend on all kind of foolishness. This is not responsible parenting. Those young people must learn the value of money. They need to work for it; otherwise they will never appreciate it. How do you expect them to be responsible adults?" he continued.

This doesn't sound like Mr. Sterling. He is always objective and fair, I thought.

46

I pulled both my ears to clear any potentially blocked airways that could have been distorting my hearing and quickly reached for my headphones as I didn't want anybody else to hear.

"Parents, loving your children is OK, but spoiling them is definitely not OK. Please, do yourselves a favour. Teach your children the value of money; teach them about budgeting and saving. Make them work for their money. Trust me, you will spare them and yourselves a lot of trouble if you do so. Young people are creative. Don't kill their creativity before they get a chance to birth some ideas and turn them into goals. I am very serious about this. It is a big issue in our nation."

Mr. Sterling took a few phone calls during his show. The first call came from a grandmother who agreed with him a hundred per cent.

"Hi, Sterling, I really appreciate your show and your objectivity. Nowadays, not many people have the guts to say things as they are. This generation doesn't know about hard work, and we as parents have only ourselves to blame. My grandparents grew up during the first World War. Life was hard. They had to feed a family of four and food was scarce, as you can imagine. My mother and her brother would leave the house early in the morning to collect anything that could be salvaged for the war effort; then her brother would walk five miles to work in an aircraft factory. My mother was a Guide girl. She

47

packaged clothing to send to the soldiers, volunteered in hospitals, and learned how to grow crops in her family allotment. This is how they contributed to the war effort. Not only did their contribution help our soldiers, but the little money my uncle earned and the vegetables and fruits my mum grew helped feed the family."

"Margaret, I appreciate you sharing this with us. This generation has no idea of the sacrifices families, including children, had to make during the war. Did your parents give you pocket money?" asked Mr. Sterling.

"Pocket money? My parents didn't give us any pocket money. It was not in their vocabulary. They didn't believe giving their children money was a due. If we wanted pocket money, they thought we should work for it. They clothed us; they fed us; they faithfully fulfilled their duty toward all of us. When we became teenagers, my siblings and I took different part-time jobs so we could earn our own money and buy little things we wanted. I have raised my own children the same way, and today each of them is hard-working. They own twenty-two properties among themselves, and money has never been a problem."

"How many children do you have, Margaret?" Mr. Sterling asked.

"I've got three children."

"So, does each of them own multiple properties?"

"Yes, my first two children own seven properties each, and the youngest owns eight."

"Good on you and your family. I hear you saying you taught your children the value of hard work, diligence, self-reliance, and it all paid off. I love it. I really love it. Margaret, thank you for phoning in. It was great to have you on our show this morning."

"It was a pleasure, Sterling. Thanks again for your show. I hope some parents learn from our experiences and stop bowing down to their children."

Oh, my word! What is the matter with Mr. Sterling today? He is a hundred per cent against me, I kept thinking.

My poor little heart started beating faster and faster. It felt as if the shock had displaced it, and it was desperately trying to run away out of fear, without me being able to do anything about it. I was sweating. I placed the headphones on the desk. The last thing I wanted was for my parents to hear Mr. Sterling's show. For a brief moment I pictured myself turning the volume down but felt completely paralysed. This weird anaesthetic was relentlessly pursuing its trajectory through my body, making my arms powerless. My tummy was rumbling like a washing machine. The lump in my throat felt heavier, and my poor legs turned into a mass of hot melted wax. I couldn't move.

Another caller phoned in.

"Hi, Sterling."

"Hi, with whom do I have the pleasure of speaking?"

"My name is Tony."

"Hi, Tony. Where do you stand on this pocket money business?"

"Well, I think we have a serious problem on our hands. I suspect the previous caller's view has been largely influenced by the war situation her grandparents experienced. Here is the other side of the argument. We live in a country where we have enjoyed peace and relative stability for decades. Resources are not scarce, and judging from the houses people live in, the cars they drive, and the holidays they can afford, it seems to me that most parents earn a decent living. They don't see why their children should work to earn their pocket money. Sometimes parents feel that because they didn't have certain things when they were growing up, they don't want their children to be deprived of them."

"You hit it on the nail, Tony. I think this is the case for many parents. They feel they ought to make life as comfortable as possible for their children. They feel guilty if they don't, especially if their children's friends receive pocket money from their parents," added Mr. Sterling.

"Yeap. It is often the case. I myself had to resist this pressure. I encouraged my teenage children to work even for two hours a week from their early teens. One did paper round, another did some babysitting for a family friend, another helped a couple of neighbours by walking their dogs, and my youngest cut the lawn for some of our neighbours."

"That is so good. How do they spend the money they earn?" Mr. Sterling asked.

"Well, they don't spend much of it. Most of it goes into their bank accounts. They use some of it to buy things they like, and they reward themselves with a little treat once in a while if you see what I mean. They also use it to buy their mother and me Christmas and birthday presents.

"Wow! Lucky you. Well, I shouldn't say 'lucky you' because your children didn't just happen to turn out to be responsible and generous. You raised them to become who they are today. Impressive, Tony, very impressive."

"They are great kids. I tell you something else, Sterling. Self-gratification in today's society is a big problem."

"You can say it again, mate."

"I do see some young people doing shift jobs to earn a bit of money, but far too many don't. One of my neighbours who is a single mother told me she has to work three extra jobs to earn extra money that she gives to her teenagers so they can buy designer clothes, shoes, and handbags."

"You're kidding me!" Mr. Sterling shouted.

"I'm not kidding. One piece of clothing costs them a hundred to two hundred pounds minimum. When I say one piece of clothing, I mean a t-shirt that doesn't look any different from what you could get on the high street. Her children won't work. They spend their time doing window and online shopping while that poor woman is working her socks off to satisfy their selfish desires," Tony continued.

"It's sad that she is encouraging her teenagers to see her as a cash machine. And let me tell you, folks, nobody feels sorry for a cash machine. All you want out of it is some cash. You need some cash, and you want the cash machine to give it to you now. And that cashpoint had better be working; otherwise you get really upset. Am I telling the truth, people? You know I am. That is how those children are treating their mother. She is a cash machine to them," Mr. Sterling restated.

I could tell he was quite upset. This was a different Mr. Sterling from the one I have known and respected.

"That's exactly how they see her and treat her. They have no compassion for her; they don't give a thought about her health or well-being. It's all about them," Tony responded.

"Yeah. Sadly, I don't find that surprising. Listen, folks, it amazes me to see how parents teach their children to be selfish. No, I'm serious. This is exactly what this mother is doing. Remember the saying: *you reap what you sow.* I am not criticising this woman. She may feel guilty that their father isn't around, and she may be seeking to compensate in every way possible. I can understand that. But Karen, Maria, Janet, or whoever you are, this is not healthy. Designer clothes, when just one item costs no less than a hundred pounds, are not a necessity. They are luxuries, and nobody should put their lives and health at risk just to wear a designer label. I hope you all hear me loud and clear."

"I'm a hundred per cent with you on this. If they want designer clothes, let them work for them," Tony added.

"Tony, thanks for phoning in. All the best to you and your children. They're heading for a brilliant future. Great talking with you."

"This is the Sterling show. Today we are talking about pocket money. Should we give our children pocket money or not? Is giving them pocket money turning them into irresponsible adults? Does encouraging our young people to work for their pocket money make them industrious? Have your say. The number to call is…." You can also comment on our social media platforms or send me an email.... Hello, with whom do I have the pleasure of speaking?"

"This is Suzy."

"Hi, Suzy. What's your view? What do you want to share with us?" inquired Mr. Sterling.

"I appreciate everything that's been said so far. I wanted your opinion on a particular point."

"We're listening to you, Suzy."

"I have two teenage children. They are twins who just turned thirteen. Some parents give their children pocket money if they help with chores around the house. I personally think children should help with housework without expecting a financial reward. They live in a house and therefore need to look after it. As parents, we need to teach our children from an early age that it is a home, not a hotel. I am not against the idea of giving children pocket money, but I am struggling with the idea of bribing them into helping around the house, if you see what I mean."

"I understand exactly what you mean. You heard Suzy. Please help her with her dilemma. Phone us, email us, or use one of our social platforms to contact us. And this is the Sterling show."

A hundred thoughts ran through my mind. Can you imagine if my parents had heard that? There would be no more pocket money. Besides, they would spread the word to my grandparents, Mummy's family, and some of our neighbours and friends who would cut the supply. They may even stop giving us birthday and Christmas presents.

Mr. Sterling has lost his mind, I couldn't help but think. *Usually he is very reasonable, and his arguments are always balanced. Until today, I have been on his side, but he has completely lost it. Maybe he has some family problems. He may well have children who have taken advantage of his kindness, and maybe what he said was really a way to pour out his heart. I quite like Mr. Sterling. I really don't know what to do. Maybe I should ask the National Society for the Prevention of Cruelty to Children to give him a call as his stance poses a serious threat to the well-being of all children. Besides, I can't believe all the callers sided with him. Mr. Sterling has a lot of influence. If a campaign to deprive us of our pocket money begins, where will it end? We will lose all our rights. The show was a complete disaster. Only time will tell of the irreparable damage it has caused to my generation and future ones.*

I spent the latter part of the afternoon thinking about the comments Mr. Sterling and the callers had made. Though I tried to put on a brave face, I knew I was not myself. Mum and Dad knew it too.

"Petite Loulou, you haven't said much this afternoon. Is anything upsetting you?" Mum asked.

What do I say? If I tell them about the show, they will want to listen to it. They might follow Mr. Sterling's advice, and it would mean the funeral of my pocket money. I need to deal with it all by myself. I just have to.

"Oh, I have been thinking about how to deal with a financial issue. I am trying to think about the best way to go about it; that's all."

"Honey, you seem to take it very seriously. Can we help you?"

"Thanks, Mummy. But there is no need. If it were something I couldn't deal with, I would rally the troops, but I can deal with it. Nothing to worry about."

"If you haven't dealt with that financial issue by tomorrow, Mummy and I would like to offer our help, all right?" Daddy added.

"Yes. I will keep both of you updated."

I rushed to the study to send Mr. Sterling an email. It had definitely not been my day. Why is it that somebody always uses the computer just when I need it? Sometimes it seems that everything is against me. Ravel had booked it until six thirty. I needed at least a full hour to write the email. By the time Mr. Sterling sees my email and gets back to me, it will be past my bedtime.

I looked at Ravel and I looked at the clock again. I could feel my throat tightening and I felt like throwing the towel. Just at that moment, Ravel said I could take his place. He completed his homework much quicker than he had anticipated. God was definitely on my side. I asked my dear brother if he could delete his name on the booking form and add

MY FAMILY, KITTEN, & ME

my name and his signature to validate my booking. I waited for him for no more than three minutes. Once he left the study, I started writing the letter.

Dear Mr. Sterling,

I hope you and your family are well.

My name is Petite Loulou. I am not a robot. I am a real person. I am somewhere between six and ten years old. I live with my parents, my siblings, Kitten, some goldfishes, and about twenty frogs whose residence is the pond in our back garden.

I regularly listen to your radio show and learn quite a lot from your talks. I even have a notepad that I use to take notes of every important thing you say.

I listened to your talk this afternoon, and, to tell you the truth, I can sense in my heart that I am angry with you. I cannot understand why you want to deprive us of our pocket money when most of us have no other sources of income.

My older sibling turned fourteen only a few months ago. She is the only one who can have a part-time job. The rest of us have to depend on our parents for our pocket money. It's the only way we can make ends meet.

I am currently working on a couple of projects to start earning money in the next five to six months. My siblings who are older than I am are also working on similar projects. I am depending on my pocket money to invest in my new projects; otherwise, I will never be able to make it in life. I

57

have awakened every morning a whole half an hour earlier to work on a new project, I have spent countless hours working on my financial plan, and I have attended and participated in a good number of business meetings.

If my parents hear that you are against parents giving their children pocket money, they will follow your advice. My siblings and I would have made all this sacrifice in vain.

We all do chores at home, but we don't see it as a favour that we do to our parents or as a means of getting paid. We help our parents because they are responsible parents, and we are responsible children. We also help the homeless people who attend our community shelter.

We do not buy designer clothes. I am very careful about what I spend my money on. I do not have a boyfriend, so I don't spend money on any presents or special meals for anyone the way Mummy and Daddy do for each other. But the day I have a boyfriend, I will tell him from the start that according to the terms of my agreement with Mr. Sterling, any boyfriend of mine has to pay for all expenses. You don't have to worry about me. I am not easily bribed. Even if he begs me, I will not spend a penny on him. You can take my word for it.

Mr. Sterling, I urge you to reconsider your position. I fear that responsible children who have a vision of what they want to achieve and a real goal will feel discouraged. Some of us may even lose hope forever.

I must tell you I have a very happy family. We have a lot of fun together. We all get on very well with each other. We don't take advantage of our parents. In reality, we are a great help to them. Now think about what would happen to this *most loving family if, because of you, my parents were to introduce the 'No pocket money bill' in our home. Think about the despair this would cause. I can tell you one thing for sure: my family would be in crisis, and you would be blamed for destroying the peace, the joy of a family, and their children's future.*

Maybe, you have not thought of this. You know how unforgiving the media and social media are and how they enjoy exposing people. Trust me; they will be all too happy to make you their next headline and ruin your career and reputation. They may even file a lawsuit. I hope you love your family enough to spare them such calamity.

I am sure a lot of politicians listen to your show. As a result of your advice, the government might make it unlawful for parents to give their children pocket money, or they might create a pocket money tax. And you and I know what would happen then. We, the taxpayers, would be the biggest losers.

As you know, not all parents can give their children pocket money, but even parents who can don't give their children a pay rise as regularly as they should. They are not mean; they simply forget. I was hoping you would appeal to those parents so they would honour their commitment to their children.

I feel that as children, the system is not in our favour. I have seen with my own eyes some parents wasting away their money on things they don't need. I have also seen some throwing things in the bin that could have been recycled. A friend of mine told me his dad has a watch for each day of the week and none of them is cheap.

My point is that instead of wasting away their money, those parents could be more generous toward their children. I wish you had said that in today's show.

For many years now, my parents have introduced a budget that is applied to the pocket money we receive. We give ten per cent to a cause that is dear to our hearts, we keep twenty per cent for our personal expenses, and we save seventy per cent. I must emphasise that I use part of my pocket money to buy presents for my parents when it is their birthday or anniversary, I also buy birthday presents for my siblings, and I always carry in my purse at least two fifty pence coins in case I meet a homeless person. Besides, my siblings and I sponsor three children in a developing country. It costs me three pounds a month. It may not sound like a lot to you, but it is a lot to me.

You can see for yourself that many people will suffer if I am no longer in a position to support them financially and demonstrate that I really care about them. So many people are counting on me. So many people believe in me. These people are not only my parents or my relatives. These are businesspeople that I meet on flights or at business conferences.

Could you please tell all your listeners that you thought about the show and you realised you didn't take into account the responsible children? Could you please make it clear that giving pocket money to children at an early age can help them better understand the value of money, and it can help them develop discipline and other life skills? Would you mind insisting on it?

Mr. Sterling, I thank you for reading my letter. My parents do not know anything about this conversation. They are extremely worried about my emotional and mental health. They do not know that today's show has hit me like a tornado. I promised them I was dealing with this issue, and I was confident it would be sorted by tomorrow.

Please, please, I really need you to get back to me with a favourable answer this evening before eight thirty so I don't have nightmares and so my parents won't worry about me, as their hearts are very fragile when it comes to their children.

Sincerely yours,

Petite Loulou

I sent the email to Mr. Sterling. I didn't know Kitten had been quietly waiting for me all along. She must have come to give me some support but didn't want to disturb me. She meowed when I opened the door, and then she stroked my legs.

"Oh, Kitten. Thank you for your solidarity. I can always depend on you. It's all done now. All we have to do is ask God to make Mr. Sterling see my email and wait for his answer. Let's go upstairs."

Kitten kept purring. She was as anxious as I was. But at least we had each other.

At around 7.40, I asked Mummy if I could borrow her laptop. I knew she would getting increasingly have reminded me of our screen curfew. We are not allowed to access mobile phones, PCs, laptops or TVs at least two hours before our bedtime. My parents take our health and well-being very seriously. I explained to Mum that I was expecting a very important email. She offered to check for me.

Ten minutes to eight. Nothing from Mr. Sterling. Five minutes past eight. Nothing. Twenty minutes past eight. Still nothing.

I was nervous. The hope I had when I emailed the letter was slowly vanishing. What if he doesn't even bother reading it? What if he's too busy or doesn't even see my email? What if he thinks I am a spoiled child who just wants to have her own way?

The more I stared at the clock, the more restless and anxious I became. Every time Mum said there was nothing, I had to rush to the toilet. That's what feeling anxious does to me. I must have burned two hundred and ten calories within those few minutes. When it was eight twenty-two, Mum said it would be my bedtime soon, and maybe the email I was expecting might arrive tomorrow. I had a dilemma. How do I come across kind of cool and, at the same time, let her know it is very important that I receive it and read it before I go to bed? I asked Mummy to keep checking and to wake me as soon as it came through. I told her Kitten would come to remind her.

Kitten came to sleep next to me. She was very supportive. When it was eight twenty-six, I asked her to go and ask Mum to check my inbox. All she needed to do was purr. She went but came back empty-handed. She jumped on my bed, waiting for my signal again. Eight twenty-eight, she went back to Mum's bedroom. Still nothing from Mr. Sterling.

I was confused. Mr. Sterling comes across as a very caring person. But suppose he is not actually caring and just pretends to be. Suppose he is a government spy, and his aim is to restore the "1984 regime" in our country, and his radio show is a coverup.

Kitten jumped off the bed without me saying anything and went to ask Mum to check again.

"I'm sorry, Kitten. There is nothing."

My heart sank. I lost hope. Kitten was leaving the room when Mummy suddenly shouted, "Kitten, there is an email for Petite Loulou. It has just come through. It's from a certain Sterling. Who is this Sterling?"

Kitten started to purr excitedly. I couldn't believe it. He had replied. I was anxious to find out what he had said. I jumped out of bed and ran to Mummy's bedroom.

"Honey, I'm glad you received your email on time. Your friend must be very reliable. You can come and read it next to me. Come," she said while making room for me to sit next to her.

"Thank you, Mummy, but I'd rather read it in my own bed."

"Are you sure?"

"Yes, Mummy," I responded as confidently as I could. I had to make sure Mr. Sterling was on my side before I showed it to her.

She gave me her laptop. "There you are then."

"Come, Kitten; let's go."

Grande Loulou was in Brigitte and Chelsea's bedroom. That was perfect timing. I sat on my bed. Kitten sat next to me, staring at the screen as if she could read. Though my hands were trembling, I managed to open the email. My eyes were wandering all over the screen, unable to remain stable. I managed to gain control of those drifting eyes just like Mummy gained control of her skidding car on the icy road last winter, and I began to read.

When I read the third line, my body gradually began to relax, my muscles were loosening up, and my breathing started to regulate. I glanced at Kitten. "Kitten, do you see what I see?"

She purred and gently touched the screen with her foot.

"Oh, sorry, Kitten. I forgot you cannot read. So far so good." With my finger, I pointed out to her how far I had gotten in the email and read it out so she could hear.

When I read the other paragraphs, I was speechless. I had not anticipated such a response from Mr. Sterling. I had to touch my face, feel the beating of my heart with my hand, and touch Kitten to ensure this was real.

"Honey, is it what you were expecting? Are you alright?" shouted Mum from her bedroom.

"No, Mummy. It's much better than I was expecting. I'm feeling terrific. I'm feeling a hundred and twenty per cent terrific. It's the best day of my life!" I shouted at the top of my voice.

"Oh, wow. I would like to share in your excitement!" she shouted.

"Kitten, from now on, my life will never be the same again. If you stick with me, you will tread where no other cats have trod. Do you hear me, Kitten? Let's go to Mummy and Daddy's bedroom."

"Meow, meow."

I rushed to my parents' bedroom with Kitten following me. "Mummy, you won't believe this. I just had my first breakthrough."

"What do you mean, honey?"

"Mr. Sterling from the Money Radio show has sent me a personal email."

"You mean Mr. Sterling, the financial expert, the guru?" she asked while straightening herself at her desk. She was so surprised.

"Daddy, Grande Loulou, Brigitte, Luke, Ravel, Chelsea, come everybody. We must have an emergency meeting right away. You've got to come now, quickly!" I shouted.

My professional career was taking off, and my siblings couldn't find anything better to do than murmur next door.

"It's Petite Loulou. I thought she was already sleeping."

"An emergency meeting at this time?"

"Right."

"She is calling 999, the home emergency team."

"There is trouble in the west wing of our house."

"Honey, what is it? Is everything OK?" Daddy shouted.

"I've just received some great news."

They all joined me in Mummy and Daddy's bedroom, curious to find out what this was all about.

"Is everybody here? Would you mind taking a seat?" I said in official way. At that point I thought of Joseph in the Bible, who, like me, had an important announcement to make to his family. His dad believed in him, but his brothers thought he was a show off. Many years later he became a prominent ruler over a foreign country, though he didn't fully understand the meaning of his dream at the time.

My siblings started to giggle and roll their eyes.

"What is it, Petite Loulou?" Grande Loulou asked impatiently.

"If it were not so late, I would have invited all of you to meet me in the sitting room to celebrate this happy occasion as it would be more appropriate. But since it's my bedtime, I have invited all of you to join me here. Mummy and Daddy, thank you for allowing me to use your bedroom."

More giggles in the camp.

"Petite Loulou, get straight to the point," said Brigitte.

"First of all, I must ask Mummy and Daddy if I could take a few minutes from my sleeping time."

"Of course, honey," Daddy said. You called an emergency meeting, so we are ready to hear what you have to say. We are-,"

"I hope you didn't call a meeting to tell us three plus three equals six," Chelsea interrupted.

They burst out laughing. At that precise moment, Kitten purred loudly and put on a serious face.

"Kitten is getting impatient. She is not impressed with your behaviour. So, let's listen to Petite Loulou," Mummy said.

"Only Kitten knows what I'm going to say. She has been my right-hand man. That's why she is calling for order."

Everybody kept quiet. I glanced at each member of my family until I had their undivided attention. "Ravel, would you mind reading this email?"

He looked to his right, then to his left. "I'll be happy to if the chair so wishes," Ravel responded while suppressing his laugh with the palm of his hand.

I walked toward him and gave him the laptop.

Dear Petite Loulou,

I trust my response to your email finds you well and that you will have a chance to read it before you go to bed this evening.

It was such an honour to receive an email from a girl as young as you, and it was a real delight to read it.

I have never received such a well-formulated and well-thought-out letter from someone as young as you in my entire career.

I want to thank you for expressing your views with such candour on today's show. I am truly honoured that you regularly listen to my radio show and find the talks inspiring.

I am deeply sorry the discussion caused you such anxiety. I cannot tell you how sad I felt when I realised the pain I had inflicted on my young listener. As soon as I read your email, I replayed today's show to find out where I had gone wrong. I was referring to young people who are over sixteen years old or who can find a part-time job but are too lazy to work. I should have made myself clear to avoid any confusion. I offer you my sincere apology.

I must, however, say that if it were not for this confusion or lack of clarity on my part, I would have never received this letter from you, and therefore I would have never known we had such a fine young lady with exceptional intellectual abilities and insight in our audience.

I must congratulate you on your resolve, your projects, and your excellent budgeting skills. I was very touched to read that you care for the homeless, and, contrary to many children, you are not only thinking about generating money, but you are also actively working toward achieving your goal.

I am very pleased you have such great parents who have instilled these important values in you and your siblings. I wish that all children could be as blessed as you are.

I would love to invite you to be my guest on one of my radio shows in the very near future so you can tell us more about your ten-, twenty-, and seventy-per cent budget plan. I think you could be a true inspiration to a lot of parents and children all around the country and abroad. I will have to ask your parents for permission, of course. I would truly be grateful if they could phone or email me so I can get in touch with them directly.

Petite Loulou, I think you have a bright future ahead of you. You can achieve great things. I don't say this lightly.

I hope you won't mind me asking you for a special favour. I would like you to be part of my circle of advisers if you and *your parents have no objection. We could discuss what this responsibility entails at a special lunch.*

I hope my letter has allayed all your anxiety and fears.

Thank you again for listening to my show and for contacting me.

I look forward to hearing from you and your parents this evening or tomorrow at your convenience.

Sterling Stewart

The Sterling Money Radio Show

When Ravel finished reading the email, the room was completely silent. But it was a silence of sublime admiration. It took a few seconds for Ravel to realise the full extent of what he had just read. He stared at me, glanced at the email, and read again, "Dear Petite Loulou."

He paused, glanced at the email again, and shouted "P-P-Petite Loulou, it's about you. Blimey!"

He threw the laptop on the bed, walked toward me, and lifted me from the floor. I remember thinking Ravel was as swift as lightning. He was beside himself. He paraded me all around the bedroom under the applause of my parents and siblings. They grabbed me, hugged me, and kissed me several times. Everybody wanted to share in this celebrity moment, and I graciously granted it, however how long they wanted it to linger on.

Daddy read the entire email all over again and stopped at each paragraph. But that was not enough. Everybody wanted to read it personally.

"Nobody is giggling now. Let this be a lesson to those concerned," Daddy stated with a light touch of humour.

Your point is well taken, Daddy," Ravel responded.

The others acquiesced.

"Daddy, was I right to call an emergency meeting?"

"Absolutely, sweetheart. You wouldn't keep this wonderful news to yourself until the morning, would you?"

"No. I couldn't wait to tell all of you."

"I'm sure you couldn't" Chelsea said.

"Petite Loulou is so confident. And dignified, I should add. You are the youngest, but you command such respect and authority," said Ravel. "I am so proud of you."

"We are all very proud of you," added Brigitte and Luke.

"Mummy's little sunshine," Mummy kept saying.

"Daddy, are you going to phone Mr. Sterling right away?"

"What would you like Daddy to do?" Daddy asked.

I would like you to phone him now. I am too excited to go to bed."

"Yes, please, Daddy," Grande Loulou said.

Mum and my siblings were excited and impatient just as I was.

"OK. But before I phoned Mr. Sterling, I would like to see…in fact, I think all of us would like to read the email you sent to Mr. Sterling."

"Oh, yes, of course. Let me look for it. This time I will read it out loud myself. May I ask you to save your comments until I have finished?"

"Consider it done, rising star," said Chelsea.

I cannot tell you how astonished my parents and siblings were while I was reading. Everyone analysed everything I had written. They were also very generous with their praise.

"Petite Loulou, you are an activist in the making. You are phenomenal!" shouted Grande Loulou.

"But I don't want to be just an activist. I am the Governor of the Bank of England, the Chancellor of the Exchequer, or the Prime Minister in the making."

"That's what I mean," added Grande Loulou.

Daddy phoned Mr. Sterling and had a very pleasant conversation with him. He told Mr. Sterling the whole family wanted to hear, so he was putting the phone on loudspeaker. Mr. Sterling kept complementing Daddy about having such a special daughter. He couldn't believe I was only eight years old. Mummy and I spoke to him too. Anyone listening to our conversation with Mr. Sterling would have thought he and I had known each other for years. We selected a date and place for our business lunch. It would be just the four of us, Mummy, Daddy, Mr. Sterling, and me, eating in a posh restaurant in London. Though my siblings felt sad that they were not invited, they were very understanding. I promised to give them a faithful account of our meeting.

"Mummy, since it will be my first official business meeting, I think I will need to wear something suitable, like a dark-coloured suit."

"I don't think you will have to, but if you would like to, we could go shopping."

"Yes, please, Mummy."

"I would like to let all of you know that Mummy and I have no intention of scrapping your pocket money. Even if Mr. Sterling had strongly advised parents not to give their children pocket money, we wouldn't have listened to him. In our home, it's Mummy and Daddy who make the rules," Daddy stated.

We all cheered.

"Considering you are all doing so well and have worked so hard to come up with your own projects,

Daddy and I thought we would help you by giving you a pocket money rise," Mummy added.

"Yeah. A fifty or sixty per cent rise would be perfect," said Luke.

"That would be perfect. We could get all our projects off the ground even sooner," added Ravel.

"Let those brand-new notes from the bank come our way. I promise you I know how I will use them," said Brigitte.

"Well, you'll find out how much at the end of the month," said Mummy.

To celebrate this special occasion, it was my privilege to choose the breakfast menu for the following day. I ordered homemade hash browns, baked beans, a selection of Nero di Toscana, Lacinato and Dazzling blue stir-fried kale, roast carrots with baby onions, toast, and fruit salad.

"We almost forgot Kitten. We must not undermine the role she played in supporting Petite Loulou. Kitten, I will fix your favourite breakfast too," Mummy said to her.

That made Kitten happy.

After my siblings had all gone to their bedroom, Mummy and Daddy wanted to have a private talk with me about the anxiety I had experienced because of the talk show. They thought I had dealt with it very well.

"I really wanted to manage the situation myself. I remembered a few strategies you had taught me. All I had to do was use them. And, eventually, they worked."

"Was the flask of warm chamomile and peppermint tea part of the strategy?" Mummy asked.

"Yes, it was, and it helped."

"But as it was coming to your bedtime, the anxiety increased, right?" Mummy said, revealing a faint smile.

"Mummy, how did you know?"

"Honey, Mummy and Daddy had been keeping an eye on you because we knew something had been bothering you. We had to make sure you could handle the situation."

"Do you think I handled my anxiety well?"

"Very well, and we are very proud of you."

"And suppose I had a hard time dealing with it?"

"Mummy and I would have stepped in and got you to tell us what the problem was. We would have talked about the issue and offer you all the comfort we could have possibly given you. We would have never let you go to bed with a heavy heart, and remember, no matter how difficult, tragic, or impossible a situation may seem, there is always a solution," Daddy said.

"Thank you for letting me deal with it on my own, but also for having plan B just in case."

We talked for only a short while because it was past my bedtime. As I was leaving my parents' bedroom, I said, "Things are happening so fast for me. Can you imagine? I will be Mr. Sterling's special guest. I will be famous."

Their eyes lit up as they smiled.

"Are you worried you will not be able to keep up with me?" I asked them.

"Honey, we've already decided if we cannot keep up with you, we will be happy to follow you," Daddy said with a witty tone in his voice.

"Mummy, I will need your help. Could you please set some time aside to tell me more about finance, business, and the economy before my appointment with Mr. Sterling?"

"I'll be happy to, honey."

When I went to bed, all I could think about was the business lunch and the show I was going to be on with Mr. Sterling.

I decided not to tell anyone at my school about my new business friend, at least not before we had our business lunch. I asked my siblings not to tell their friends either. I needed some private time to come to terms with my new status.

CHAPTER FIVE

A SPECIAL GUEST ON THE STERLING MONEY RADIO SHOW

It took four weeks for Sunday to come; that's how it felt. Our business lunch was terrific. Meeting Mr. Sterling in person, having lunch with him, and discussing our next radio show was awesome. He and I just jelled. Mum and Dad got on very well with him too. He was the kindest person I had ever met, and he could be very funny. We talked about so many things. It made me realise how knowledgeable and intelligent my parents were. It is so important to have parents who don't cause you any embarrassment. I cannot tell you how important it is to make a good impression. I am very proud of both of them.

When I told Mr. Sterling I had wondered if he was a spy, he laughed so much. He thought I had a vivid imagination.

Oh, I should tell you that I looked very smart in my new dark blue jacket. I made quite an impression on Mr. Sterling. He asked Mum where she had bought my jacket because he would have liked to buy one for his own daughter. I felt truly honoured. You see, I have known all along that if I wanted to be taken seriously, I had to look the part. If I had the time, I could start my own fashion line for girls and teach them how to dress to command respect, but fashion is not really my thing.

When we got back home around six in the evening, my siblings, and grandparents who had been babysitting, couldn't wait to hear about our business lunch. When I told them I was going to be on the show in two weeks, they were all so excited. I gave them permission to tell their friends.

Before lunchtime the following day, the entire school knew I was going to be Mr. Sterling's guest. It was very kind of Mrs Buckle to inform the pupils. I suspect she may have thought I would mention our school and she would get some credit and maybe even a grant or some donation as a result. But my school had no part to play in my rise to fame. My parents are the ones who deserve the credit.

The day I was going to be Mr. Sterling's special guest finally arrived. When I woke up that Sunday, I had expected that a tsunami of anxiety would be pushing and pulling me in all directions since my classmates had advised me to expect it. But it was nothing like that. I said my prayers and told myself there was no reason to fear. I felt calm and composed. If there was any mean caller on the show, I would tell him or her exactly what I thought and move on to the next caller.

When we got to the radio station, a lovely lady came and escorted us to the VIP lounge where we had some tea and snacks. We were introduced to at least a dozen staff members who seemed to be delighted to meet us. Mr. Sterling came to greet us and showed my parents and siblings the room where they would be watching me. Then he and I walked toward the studio where I was going to be live on the air. Though it was my first time in a studio, the surroundings somehow felt familiar. Finally, the moment arrived.

"Good morning, London, good morning England, France, Africa, America, the Caribbean, Singapore, Australia, and wherever you are. This is the Sterling Money Show, the only show that seeks to educate and empower you, so you learn to make smart choices and make your pennies and pounds, or whatever your currency is, work for you. Thanks again for your emails, tweets, comments, and questions on our different platforms. I have a very special show for you today. If you haven't gathered your children and teenagers around the family table or on the sofa to listen to today's show, I strongly advise you to get them to listen, for this show may change their lives," Mr. Sterling started.

"Last week I promised we would have a very special guest on today's show. She is here with us. But before I introduce her, I want to give you a bit

79

of background. You will remember that a couple of weeks ago, we did a show on pocket money. Little did I know that in our audience was a young girl who was attentively listening. Subsequently, I received an email from her, to which I had to reply immediately. With her permission and that of her parents, I would like to read you the email."

Mr. Sterling read my email, then proceeded to introduce me. I could see my family cheering me on through the big glass. Mr. Sterling had told me we would focus on five main areas: (1) why I thought it was important to give children pocket money and when it was not a good idea; (2) what my parents have taught my siblings and me about money; (3) why financial education is important from an early age; (4) my ten-, twenty-, and seventy-per cent budget plan and the projects I am currently working on; and (5) my advice to parents, children, and schools.

I was overwhelmed by the encouragement and compliments I received from the callers. I told them about my daily routine and the projects my siblings and I have been working on. I was particularly pleased that young people phoned in to say how thankful they were. Quite a few of them made the decision to make better use of their pocket money. In addition, more than twenty young people said they will no longer accept pocket money from their parents, because they were going to find part-time jobs and contribute to their household while saving money for something worthwhile.

Several parents also decided they would empower their children instead of giving them money as if they were giving their children food vouchers. No less than thirty-eight parents admitted that though they supported a charity or two, they had not taught their children to do the same, but they were going to rectify that.

Mr. Sterling was extremely pleased. He had tears in his eyes when he thanked me. I remember him saying on the air, "Petite Loulou, I am so grateful for your presence and contribution to today's show. It all started because of the email you sent me. I cannot tell you how grateful I am to you, your parents, and your siblings. I hope you realise how much our audience has appreciated your contribution to this programme. We have never had so many children and young people phone in or contact us via social media. And we have never had a topic that created so much unanimity. We have a thank-you present for you. It is a personalised glass octagon award. I hope you like it."

"Oh, Mr. Sterling, it is so beautiful," I said. "I like the way my name along with the Sterling Money Radio Show has been engraved. I will cherish it for the rest of my life. I would like to say a big thank you to you and to the staff members who have been very kind to me and my family. I would also like to express my gratitude to the audience. It's been an honour to be on your show and talk to so many young people and their parents. Feel free to contact me if you need any help."

"I am pleased to hear that, Petite Loulou. It's been such a delight to have you on our show. We would like you to come back for another show, and we hope you will accept our invitation. Thank you to all our listeners, to those of you who phoned in or who have contacted us through social media. This was the Sterling Money Radio Show on this beautiful Sunday afternoon. See you next week, same time, same place."

I was the star of my family as well as the star in my neighbourhood, my school, and everywhere I was known. People recognised me on the streets and in shops and paid me a lot of compliments. As I write these lines, I am still receiving thank-you notes from people all around the world. Some people have sent me money to help with my projects. I am so touched by their generosity. I didn't know there were so many good people in the world. Why do the bad people get all the attention in the media? Why don't we give more airtime to the good people who make a positive difference in this world?

I had been looking forward to being on Mr. Sterling's Radio Show so much. I thought I was going to feel like a celebrity because many people had told me that's how I would feel. But the thing I loved best about being on the show was hearing parents and young people say I had helped them. I cannot find the right words to express how I feel, but maybe you'll understand if I tell you it gave me a sense of purpose, it made me feel I could help others, and I felt so much joy in giving a little bit of what I had. I now look at the world differently. Every morning I ask myself how I can make a difference in somebody's life, even in your life as you read these lines.

CHAPTER SIX

SERIOUSLY TAKING OFF

I often hear famous people say that being a celebrity comes with a cost. I thought it was a gross exaggeration until I had experienced it first-hand.

You know how Kitten doesn't like to be upstaged. She realised Mr. Sterling would phone me often whereas he didn't phone her once. Whenever she would hear his name, she would start making all sort of loud noises. I would move to a different room to be in a quiet space, and sure enough, she would follow me and purr as loud as she could. On one occasion, Luke and Ravel had to keep her in their bedroom. Another time, Caleb had to keep her in the kitchen. When I would finish talking with Mr. Sterling and come out of the room, she would hit me with her tail, tell me off, and walk away. She wouldn't talk to me for a good couple of hours. But I never retaliated.

I, however, felt that I had to tell her she was jealous and immature, and it was time she grew up. I reckon that it was my fault, at least partly. I would often call her to come next to me so that together we could listen to the recording of my show with Mr. Sterling. I never knew that deep down she was harbouring such feelings of jealousy and animosity toward me.

It was also clear she was developing some kind of dislike to Mr. Sterling. I thought she wanted the best for me as I've always wanted the best for her. I wouldn't want to label Kitten as the bad apple in our family because she has many qualities, but I am concerned about our future relationship. If her attitude persists, I will have to set some strong boundaries. I will feel a bit sad for my parents who do all they can to foster harmony and peace between every member of our family. It will break their hearts to realise that Kitten is turning into a bad apple.

Although Mum works from home, she regularly goes to conferences to give seminars or to deliver training courses. She showed us an overview of the next conference she is attending as a guest speaker in a couple of weeks. I wish I could attend those seminars too: *How to be Mortgage-Free in Ten Years or Less*, *How to Multiply Your Assets and Decrease Your Liabilities*, *How to Create Wealth*, and a host of other things. Just what I needed. After dinner I went to the conservatory with the program of the upcoming seminar to have a chat with mummy. She was watering her succulents and cacti.

"Mummy, the programme looks very interesting, but it is unfortunate that it's only for adults. I'm sure many children would have liked to attend the conference, but there is nothing in the programme that is tailored for children my age, and that is why most of us will be poor throughout our whole working lives and even after we have retired."

"Honey, don't be so pessimistic."

"But think about it. If those conferences were designed with us in mind, whole schools and home-educated children would be attending too. We would all be money wise. Every child would have a personal financial plan, and by the time we turn twenty, we may not be rich, but we would not be poor. We would be mortgage-free at twenty-eight, and by the time we reach forty, we would have so many investments we could retire and invest our time in other projects."

"I couldn't agree more."

"I suppose it's too late to contact the conference manager and ask if he could accommodate children. The conference is in two weeks, isn't it, Mummy?"

"It is far too late. And it is fully booked I'm afraid."

"Would you mind speaking to the conference manager and telling him I would be interested in attending the next conference? Please ask him to schedule it during the next school break. I also promised Daddy I would take him with me. I'm sure all of us would want to attend."

"You can count on me, honey," she responded.

"Thank you, Mummy darling."

After I spoke to mum, I explained to Kitten that mummy was going to be very busy over the next two weeks and she should try to be on her best behaviour as not to cause her any undue stress. She promised she would do her best and I promised to give her an extra serving of her favourite food as a reward. I was about to share with her what I had learned about Operant Conditioning, but I soon gave up the idea; I concluded she mind try to bribe me once she would know how it works. I added that if she needed additional support for one reason or another during this period, she could come to me.

On the day of the seminar Mum and Auntie Eileen left very early. Auntie Eileen accompanied her this time. By the time Grandad and Grandma arrived that morning, we were all ready, except Daddy.

When Kitten heard their voices, she ran to them and behaved as if she had not eaten anything that morning. We told them Kitten had her breakfast before we did and that she was not hungry. She would have never asked for extra if she hadn't seen Grandad feeding a couple of birds. At first, Grandad resisted Kitten's plea, but Kitten made him feel so bad that he just gave in. Grandma told Grandad that he was too soft and that Kitten had him wrapped around her little paw.

Kitten didn't care what Grandma thought or said to Grandad. All she cared about was having another serving. And she knew she could take advantage of Grandad.

"Her mother is gone for the day. She misses her. You know that Kitten is not the greedy type. It's comfort eating," Grandad stated in his defence.

Once Daddy got ready, he came downstairs and found Kitten eating again. He kissed his parents good morning, then glanced at Grandad and said, "It looks as if Dad fell for it again."

Upon this, Grandma went on about how Grandad had to toughen up. She told him she pities him if she dies before he does. She told Dad that if she goes before he does, he will have to keep an eye on Grandad because he will easily be fooled, and if he couldn't stand up to Kitten, she couldn't see how he would be able to stand up to anyone. Daddy tried to reassure Grandma, but she stood her ground.

"Grandma, there is no need to worry. I will look after Grandad because I know how to manage him," I stated.

"There you see, my darling," Grandad hurried to say, "Petite Loulou will look after me. That should give you complete peace of mind. And you know how much I love you. I will be sure to follow all your instructions if you go before me." He laughed, wrapped his arms around her, and gave her a big kiss. This irritated Grandma even more. We love it when Grandad teases Grandma. In fact, we encourage him to tease her. It is like watching a live comedy.

Grandma and Grandad took us to school and came for us after school and took us to our music lessons. When we got home, dinner was ready, and the table was set. All in all, they cope quite well with their grandchildren.

Daddy collected Mummy and Auntie Eileen from the conference centre. When they arrived, the three of them looked very excited. Though they attributed it to their productive day, I suspected there was more to it, but I couldn't work out the real reason.

At the dinner table, Mummy and Auntie Eileen gave us a summary of the seminars. They brought lots of booklets too. We were grateful but we wanted to be there.

"I know you wanted to attend the conference today, but I'm sure you will be able to attend one day," said auntie Eileen.

"One day? You mean when we are sixteen?" Luke said.

"No, honey. I was thinking in the near future."

"I tell you what we should do. We should disguise ourselves as adults and go to the next conference," Grande Loulou said in jest.

"Excellent idea," said Caleb. "And if they try to refuse us entrance, all we have to do is to throw a big tantrum, threaten to call the media, and remind them of our rights."

"We could also threaten to go on a hunger strike. That would definitely work," continued Ravel.

Once all of us had expressed our disappointment as well as our desire to attend the next conference, Mummy declared that she forgot something and asked to be excused from the table. When she returned a minute or so later, she handed me a sealed envelope with my name written on it.

"Thank you, Mummy. What is it?" I asked.

"Why don't you open it and see for yourself?" she responded.

"Petite Loulou, read it aloud so we can all hear," said Caleb.

"Did you send another email to Mr. Sterling?" asked Chelsea.

"Have you told somebody off again?" Grande Loulou asked.

"Now, we never know what to expect when there is a phone call or a letter for Petite Loulou," Ravel commented.

"You can say that again," Luke emphasised.

Suddenly, Brigitte rose from her seat, and with her most authoritative voice and uncompromising demeanour, she addressed my siblings, "Order in the house, ladies and gentlemen. Order. Let the honourable Petite Loulou read her letter. I will not have this house being an embarrassment to the public and the laughingstock of the media. Order. I need complete silence in the house, and silence we shall have. Now, Petite Loulou, you may proceed."

Brigitte took all of us by surprise. I couldn't proceed because we all burst out in hysterical laughter. Our body temperatures rose in a flash, colouring our faces with a red brush. Our convulsive bodies could not sit still. Tears succumbed to the pressure of our lacrimal glands, Mum had to hold her tummy to avoid an embarrassing accident, and Grandad hobbled his way to the toilet.

Kitten, who was quietly seated on the chair, jumped. She looked around and jumped down. She didn't know what to do next. When she realised there was no danger, that we were just laughing away, she jumped back up on the chair, curled up, and closed her eyes.

As soon as we managed to bring our emotions under control, Grandma and Grandad commented that they had never seen such a happy bunch of comedians like their grandchildren. After several aborted attempts, I managed to read the letter.

"Dear Petite Loulou,

I trust my letter will find you well.

My name is Steve Connells. I am the event coordinator for the next conference.

More than three years ago, your mum suggested I incorporate seminars for young people in our conferences. Though the idea was appealing, we didn't think it would generate a lot of interest.

Recently, I had the pleasure of listening to Mr. Sterling's radio show where you were a guest. I was blown away by your knowledge, your passion to see young people educated in financial matters, as well as the projects you and your siblings are currently working on. Since this show aired, we have also received a substantial number of emails from parents, young people, and educators who have asked if we could organise seminars for young people and if we could invite you and your siblings to be among the presenters.

Our next conference is scheduled in October during half-term. We would be honoured if you and your siblings would present a seminar over those two days. We will discuss the details with you and your family.

I look forward to hearing from you soon.

Steve Connells

Event Coordinator

I had to read the letter twice, even three times, to ensure I had correctly understood what I had just read. I had to make sure my mind was not playing tricks on me. The whole family was ecstatic. Everyone put down their cutlery for fear of missing out on a word or a sentence. The only thing I could hear was the sound of my voice competing with the strong smell of vegetable curry.

When I had finished reading, I shouted, "Oh, wow!" I must have repeated "Oh, wow!" at least five times, each time lounder, like a piece of music that rises to a crescendo.

All I was asking was for those conferences to be open to young people. I got more than I had bargained for. It was hard to imagine that my siblings and I were guest speakers. It felt surreal.

The content of this letter created a whole new dynamic at our dinner table that evening. I don't have time to fill you in with all the details; otherwise, I will not be able to hand in my homework to Miss Barker in a couple of days. But I'm sure it will not be difficult for you to imagine how our conversation unfolded as well as the compliments that were paid to me. Grandad and Grandma were happy to be there that evening to experience this moment live instead of having an account of it.

I said good night to Kitten. For the sake of our relationship, I decided I wouldn't tell her about the invitation I had just received.

When it was my bedtime, Daddy came to tuck me in. I had something on my heart that I needed to share with him. "Daddy, I had promised that when I reach the top, I will help you reach the top too. You are not jealous because I'm helping my siblings reach the top first, are you?"

"Oh, honey, how could I be jealous? I am so happy for all of you. I am a very proud father. You will be able to help so many other young people and their parents. Reaching the top is not just about how much money you have in your bank account or how many followers you have on Facebook, Twitter, or Instagram. It's about reaching out to help somebody, and each one can certainly reach one."

"If I can make a difference, even a small one, that will matter more to me than anything else. But I also want to make a lot of money to live a comfortable life and be in a position to help children."

"That's my girl. So, how many kisses would my princess like this evening?"

"Seven."

Daddy gave me a kiss on my forehead, one on my chin, and two on each cheek.

"Daddy, you only gave me six kisses. One is missing."

"Oh, dear. How could I miss one?" he asked with a zest of humour. "Well, in that case, I have to start all over again."

"Daddy, you missed two this time."

"I'm so sorry. I definitely have a numeracy problem."

He then covered me with kisses. We both giggled.

"Sweet dreams, sweetheart. I love you."

"Sweet dreams, Daddy. I love you too."

Daddy did the same to Grande Loulou. We love when he pretends he cannot count and uses it as an excuse to shower us with big heart-shaped kisses.

When we woke up the next morning, we felt reinvigorated. This new burst of energy gave a new rhythm to all our activities for the next few weeks. We had a forthcoming business meeting with Steve Connells, a seminar to prepare, and new deadlines.

The self-appointed boss had it all worked out. We would use our family breakfast time to exchange ideas and write down any ideas that popped into our heads. Then we would have our first planning meeting for the conference on Sunday morning. Once we had written the structure for our seminar, we would email it to Mr. Connells for feedback. Then we would work on the content. Chelsea would focus on the illustrations, Luke and Ravel would work on the booklet, Caleb would select and edit photographs of all of us, Grande Loulou would work on our biographies, I would liaise with Mr. Connells, and Mum and Dad would be our advisors.

I emailed Mr. Connells the structure and an overview of our presentation. I submitted a short biography and photographs of each of us as well as our booklet template.

About two weeks after I received his invite, we all met with him and two of his colleagues. They were thrilled with our accomplishments. They explained in detail how the conference would run. Mummy and Daddy had to sign a consent form. We would be presenting two seminars in the morning and two in the afternoon over two days, but I would be the main speaker. My siblings would essentially be supporting speakers for the lead speaker. And we would be getting paid. That makes us true professionals. Talking about rising stars.

Mr. Sterling would be attending the conference too as one of the guest speakers. To share the platform with him at such a big event is truly an honour. If it were not for him, my family and I would still be in the shadows.

My best friend, Sharleen, kept asking when I was going to tell the class that my siblings and I were guest speakers at the conference.

I gently reminded her that true professionals have a spokesperson or somebody in charge of marketing, and that I wished she would have been capable enough to take on this responsibility, because she is my best school friend, but I didn't think she was suitable for such a demanding post.

She was in total agreement. Then I told her that Mr. Connells' marketing team would send invites to the head of our school and the head of my siblings' school. She was glad that our school was going to be invited.

Everything we needed for our seminars was finalised several weeks before the beginning of the conference. There was, however, one small but important detail we had to take care of as the days were flying by: what we would wear. This topic divided us into two camps. The boys thought that we were too fussy, that we had plenty of clothes, and there was absolutely no need to waste our money on buying new clothes for the occasion. They gave us a lecture on the importance of wise investing and the danger of being over-preoccupied with self-image.

We argued that buying a necessary item of clothing was a good investment. I agreed with them, but I also agreed with my sisters until Brigitte, Chelsea, and Grande Loulou pointed out that Mummy had bought me a jacket for the business lunch with Mr. Sterling, so they were entitled to a new piece of clothing too. I felt I was being used in support of their argument, but I thought it best not to express my feelings in the presence of the boys.

We eventually came to an agreement. The boys offered to look at our wardrobes, and we looked at theirs. If any of us thought that one of us, or all of us, needed another item of clothing, we would be honest enough to say so.

We started by scanning the boys' wardrobes. Then the boys scanned ours. After some deliberation, we reached a consensus that Caleb and Luke didn't need extra clothes, but that Ravel needed a new shirt, Chelsea and Grande Loulou needed a new pair of trousers and a jacket, and Brigitte and I had need of nothing.

We reported our findings to the members of the jury, that is, Mum and Dad, but they had to see the evidence for themselves. They agreed with us, except they thought Ravel needed two new shirts, not just one. He had grown a lot over the last few weeks.

I must say that my siblings and I are good at teamworking and problem solving. We may complain, grumble, and even show a bit of resistance at times, but our team spirit always prevails in the end.

Gigantic posters of the conference wallpapered the billboards, details were available on social media, and invites were sent to schools as well as to various youth and children's organisations. Our photograph and a caption that read *with special guests, Petite Loulou and her siblings,* brought the poster to life.

By the time we arrived at school on that wet and windy Monday, everybody knew that my siblings and I were going to be guest speakers at the conference. In fact, it was the topic of conversation on the school playground, in the classrooms, and in the canteen, not only on that day, but on subsequent days. This buzz was not only the result of the posters and invites, however.

The day before, Mr. Sterling had told his audience that we were going to be guest speakers at the conference in October during half-term, and they should purchase their tickets as soon as possible to avoid disappointments. Many of our school friends' parents listen to his radio show, so the word spread like wildfire.

The invite had reached the headmistress' office, and it was reported that she was over the moon. She had been heard stating that finally her commitment and hard work had paid off, and her school was finally getting the recognition it deserved. She apparently convened a staff meeting early in the morning with key staff members to discuss how they could take advantage of these circumstances to give the school maximum exposure.

From what I heard, their discussion revolved around status, image, and money. I wouldn't have believed this if I hadn't heard it with my own two ears from Mrs Buckle herself, when we were in her office. Besides me, she had invited Caleb and Grande Loulou, who now, thanks to me, had reached celebrity status. She congratulated herself and us on our achievement and said how happy she was that we had made the school proud. She confessed she had longed for this day for many years, but now that she was so close to retirement, she had resigned herself to the fact that it might never happen.

We listened to her with great interest, especially when she said that Halleydale Primary School will go down in history as a top school that births prodigies. She added that now, with such publicity, the school had earned its right to a more substantial grant from the local authority, and some generous entrepreneurs might feel impressed to make a large donation.

At that point, I thought to myself that Mrs Buckle was changing my script to write her own, and on top of that, she was using my name without my permission. The three of us kept looking at each other. I knew from the look on Caleb' and Grande Loulou's faces that we were thinking the same thing.

We asked her what she would do if she was given this substantial grant. She replied she would refurbish the staff room, buy a new photocopier, and replace some old furniture. When she said a more modern touch was long overdue, her countenance really lit up.

"Mrs Buckle, our school has taught us a lot of things, but our parents are the ones who have taught us about the value of money and who are actively involved in our projects. Last year, when they asked if you would allow us to take a day off from school to attend an important conference as part of our financial education, you made a big fuss," Caleb stated.

"Really, you shouldn't take credit for something you didn't do," Grande Loulou added.

"Mrs Buckle, if I were in your shoes and got a grant, instead of refurbishing the school, I would put a project in place so the pupils could learn about finance," I added.

We could tell she was feeling uncomfortable. Her excitement was gone, and her disappointment only accentuated the wrinkles around her eyes and upper lip. The room was quiet except for the whisper of the wind that travelled at its leisure into her office.

When we left, Caleb murmured there was no way he would have allowed her to take the credit due to Mum and Dad. Grande Loulou rightly remarked that we might be kind, but we are not naïve. I told them it felt as if I had written a great piece of music and somebody else collected the royalties.

Do not get me wrong. Mrs Buckle is a nice person. Maybe she just got carried away or got caught in a daze of excitement that clouded her mind.

As you can see, being a celebrity also has its share of disadvantages. While Mrs Buckle and a few staff members' claim to fame was that we attended

Halleydale Primary School, our schoolmates and the public treated us as if we were Father Christmas. My classmates wanted me to give them a special discount on their tickets and reserve the best seats for them at the conference. The secondaries experienced the same thing in their school. Brigitte, Chelsea, Luke, and Ravel reported to us that, just like we had to set the record straight in our school, they had to do the same in theirs.

It is only fair to say that staff and pupils were proud of us. We had more friends than we had ever hoped to have or that we could cope with. Sharleen was the only friend to whom I gave a VIP ticket. I have learned from my parents that we do not turn our backs on our best friends because we fly a little higher than they do. I promised Sharleen I would be her best friend as long as I live. The poor thing breathed a sigh of relief. I could almost hear her heartbeat.

When we got home, we found no less than twenty best-wishes cards from our neighbour friends. Some of them came around to share in the excitement. Most people living on our street knew about it and promised to attend the conference, our seminars in particular. That was so generous of them.

CHAPTER SEVEN

THE COST OF BEING FAMOUS

I promised myself I would not say a word to Kitten, but it felt as if I was hiding something from her; it felt as if I was being dishonest, and I did not feel good about that. I am sure you'll understand. So, I had to find a way to tell her without running the risk of stirring more jealousy in her and getting upset with all of us.

When we received the posters from Mr. Connells, my siblings wanted to post them on our bedroom wall, in the study, and in the hallway. I asked them to hide the posters from Kitten's view and not to mention a word to her until I had a chance to speak to her.

The following day, soon after dinner, I approached Kitten and congratulated her on the little things she had recently done and on her general appearance. I told her how proud we were of her for being so grown up and for displaying such impeccable behaviour. I gave her lots of affirmation. I never once mentioned any incidents that you and I know about. I followed the advice given by psychologists and counsellors to the letter, and it worked. Kitten felt really good about herself. She kept meowing and rolling over on her back while I was talking to her. I knew I had her attention and trust.

"Kitten, there is something I have to tell you."

She raised her head and looked at me straight in the eyes.

"You are not in a hurry or anything like that, are you?"

"Meow."

"OK. Well, you may have noticed that all of us have been very busy lately. Well, I mean we have been busy in a different way. Do you remember when I was on the…"

I was really close to saying "Sterling Show," but I stopped in the nick of time because I knew she would have gotten really angry.

"I meant I was on one of those programmes. Well, I have another programme coming up. This time it will be all of us, except Mum and Dad."

Kitten was looking increasingly curious and agitated too.

"It's nothing phenomenal. Well, it's a bit phenomenal, but trust me; it's a lot of hard work and a lot of responsibility. You wouldn't want to be in our shoes; trust me."

I paused for a few seconds and watched her every move to assess her behaviour. I felt I had a green light, so I continued, "Yeah, so I was saying that you're really lucky to be able to manage your time as you please. You don't have to worry about seminars, cash flow, the financial markets, investing in the right business for a good return, brokers, or trading. You have no idea how lucky you are.

"Meow, meow."

"And listen; that's not all. You know that nowadays, some dishonest people can steal people's identities. They can even trace where you live and kidnap you. Our world is no longer safe, you know. When people have their photographs on social media, on an invite, or worst of all, on a poster, their very lives are at stake."

Kitten stood up on all fours and looked quite frightened. She was completely oblivious to what was happening in the real world.

"We have our photograph on a poster. I will show it to you. But trust me; you wouldn't want to have yours on that poster. It is too big a risk, far too big."

Kitten looked relieved. I stroked her, waited a little bit to ensure that I could go ahead, and then asked, "Would you like to see the invite now?"

"Meow, meow."

I got up and fetched the invite. She followed my every move.

"OK, there it is. What do you think?"

She looked at the poster, put her front feet on the photograph, and glanced at me.

"Yeah, as I told you, it is a big risk we are taking. It takes a lot of guts to have ourselves so exposed, enough to cause us sleepless nights and even give us nightmares. At least you do not have to worry. You are safe. We would never put you through this."

Kitten kept looking at me. I was wondering if she wanted her photograph on the invite like the rest of us. Was she upset? I was prepared for the green light to turn to amber and then to red. I started to sweat. My heart was pounding. She stared at the invite. Not one purr.

After about a minute, she started to perforate our photograph with her claws, then jumped from the sofa, walked toward the bin, and dumped us. She came back, sat next to me, and spread herself on the sofa. My eyes were swelling with tears.

I was speechless. I had never imagined I would witness such a cold act toward me and my siblings. I did not want to betray my feelings, so I sat still, fighting back those tears until I could do so no longer. I rushed to the toilet, ran the tap, and allowed myself to silently cry.

That night, I went to bed with a heavy heart. No one had never torn my photograph. I did not know how to interpret this merciless gesture from Kitten. All I knew was I had been reduced to a piece of rubbish.

The following morning, Mum saw the poster in the bin and asked why it had been torn and dumped. I told her of my conversation with Kitten the night before and asked her not to make a big fuss about it. Kitten was out during breakfast, which gave us a chance to freely speak of the incident. Caleb promised to design a similar template and add her picture to avoid any unpleasant surprise.

I had never realised how toxic sibling rivalry could become. You may have all the wisdom and the best intentions and treat every member of your family with love, but that is never a guarantee that everyone will rejoice over your success. I cannot tell you how much I needed my family's support to help me deal with Kitten's animosity.

Daddy said that what Kitten did was a precursor of what would happen during and after the conference and told us we had better prepare ourselves to see our posters and the invites torn apart and thrown in the bin, but we shouldn't take it personally. I felt so much better after we talked about it. I just had to brace myself.

Telling you about myself and my family is one of the most difficult things I have done in my entire life. Whenever a celebrity writes an autobiography, I would imagine it is always a challenge to decide what to include and what to leave out. The last thing you want is to come across as boastful or blowing your own trumpet.

I could easily have told you that my neighbours were queuing up almost every day to have a VIP chat with us—with me, really. Or I could list all the radio stations and TV channels that have invited me on their shows, or the hundreds of requests I have received for autographs. I could have also told you that my reputation has travelled across Europe and other parts of the world, that I have also been featured on the covers of top magazines, and that my producer is currenting editing my latest CDs and DVDs, but this is not necessary.

Many of my schoolmates kept asking me if the Prime Minister or the Chancellor of the Exchequer had contacted me yet. I told them I did not expect them to contact me so soon. It must be difficult for them to come to terms with the reality that by inviting me, they are inviting their young successor. They must find it very intimidating. I told them if I did not hear from their office by next month, I would consider dropping them both a line, and I would do the same for the Governor of the Bank of England, to invite myself. I think it is in the best interest of the country that I seek to alleviate their fears and offer my expertise.

As I am writing these lines, my personal assistants are negotiating my fees for future speaking engagements, both here and abroad; I leave it to my parents to take care of these details so I can focus on my seminars and projects. It is also good for them to get so involved.

The other day, while I was relaxing on the sofa in the conservatory, sipping some fresh mint, ginger, and lemon tea, a strange thought came to my mind. Your parents help you take your first steps in life, but before you know it, you are the one guiding their steps so they may climb a little higher and get a panoramic view of life. Who would have thought that I would be the one paving the way for my whole family? Talk about the irony of life.

Finally, the day of the conference came. The venue was gigantic. The seminar rooms were furnished with high-tech equipment that obeyed our command at the push of a button. We arrived early to re-familiarise ourselves with the place and to set up. We had two staff members allocated to us for the two days. The crowd increased by hundreds every minute. We could feel the buzz in the massive hall. The place was teeming with people of different ages, races, and nationalities. Every member of my family had a VIP badge. Our grandparents, aunties, uncles, neighbours, friends, Mum and Dad's colleagues, pupils from both our schools, and staff members had come to offer their support and learn from us.

I was so glad when I saw Mr. Sterling and Mr. Connells. They are not just professional colleagues to me. They are also friends to me and my family.

Sharleen arrived as we were just about to go backstage. She ran toward me, hugged me, and said it was my time to shine. Our parents hugged us and reminded us where they would be seated so we could look at them if we needed a bit of encouragement. I said a silent prayer. Then the moment everyone had been waiting for had finally arrived.

"Ladies and Gentlemen, boys and girls, young people, it gives me great pleasure to welcome our youngest seminarists," announced Mr. Connells. "Please, put your hands together and give them a warm, encouraging welcome."

Upon his announcement, my siblings and I made our way to the stage, where we were introduced to the seven hundred attendees in the hall. Any trace of nervousness faded as we spoke, especially since our PowerPoint presentation looked ten times better on the giant screen. I felt increasingly relaxed as I kept speaking, and it felt great to share information that could make a big difference in the life of my audience.

After I spoke, it was Ravel's turn. He did so well I thought there was no way our other siblings could do better. But every one of them excelled. I was so proud of them.

When we concluded the first seminar, the crowd stood as one and showered us with applause for a good while. If Mr. Connells had not come to remind them we had less than fifteen minutes for Q&A, they would still be cheering us.

At the end of our first seminar, no less than fifteen children with limited mobility or learning disabilities told Caleb he had given them hope. Caleb told them they should never allow their limitations to define them and that our perspective determines the trajectory as well as the quality of our lives. They felt truly encouraged and asked if Caleb could be their friend. Caleb said to us that nothing impacted him more than the children and teenagers who told him how much he had been an inspiration to them. I suspect he will be mentoring them.

Mrs Buckle had a change of heart. She came to us and showered us with compliments. She was also very generous with her congratulations to my parents. As I told you, she is a lovely headmistress, who, like all of us, had an ego moment at a most unfortunate time. All is forgiven. All is forgotten.

The other three seminars on the first day went as well as the first one. Many children and their parents were not content with attending our seminar once; they came back to repeat our seminar the same day and even the following day.

The second day went quickly. We were more confident and far more relaxed. Mr. Sterling attended the second seminar and was very impressed with our presentation. Mr. Connells' thank-you speech to us brought the house down. Parents had tears in their eyes, and children wanted to touch us to find out if we were real.

A total of eight seminars over a two-day conference, countless autographs, one-to-one chats and pictures with fans and professionals, as well as hundreds of kisses and hugs from family members and friends had left us all exhausted. Seminars delivered. Mission accomplished. One hundred per cent successful. It was time to say goodbye to all the staff and those who had offered their best wishes and support.

We all got on the minibus that Daddy had hired for the occasion and waved goodbye to this amazing venue. Before Daddy drove away, we looked back at the venue one last time, and Grande Loulou and I said in unison, "See you next year. We will be back."

I wanted to take a moment to recall the events over the two days and express my gratitude for our success, but neither my body nor my spirit was up for it. I drifted off to sleep as soon as Daddy drove past the building.

When we got up the following day and went to the dining room for breakfast, four national newspapers with our photograph on the front page were on the table. Our inbox was inundated with emails. Our Twitter and Facebook pages, and even our letter box, had experienced a thousand times more traffic. What a proud moment! What a humbling experience!

You may wonder what Kitten's reaction was at the end of the conference. That's a long story. Kitten will always be Kitten. I will fill you in next time. As you can deduce, I have far more responsibility and a tight schedule. So, please, do send me a note to remind me.

P.S.

Dear Miss Smith,

It gives me great pleasure to submit the second part of my homework. Thank you again for your positive feedback concerning the first one. The third part will follow.

I must ask a favour of you. I have included sensitive information about our school, namely Mrs Buckle. I would very much appreciate if you would keep to yourself the paragraph referring to the private conversation Mrs Buckle, my siblings, and I had in her office. Although everything I said is true, I would not want to cause her any embarrassment. When a senior staff member is so close to retirement, she has earned the right to have her dignity protected.

Let me thank you for coordinating the seminars for our school. As previously mentioned, the suggested dates are perfect. Do let me know if there are any specific points you would like me to address besides the ones mentioned. As you requested, I have given more thought to the school's offer to pay for my seminars. My position remains the same: my seminars for our school are free of charge. Nevertheless, if our school wishes to make a contribution, I will be much happier if you create a fund that will help the disadvantaged children in our school.

I am delighted that my humble effort has helped raise the profile of our school, and, as a result, a substantial number of donors have given so generously to our school.

Lastly, I just want to say how much I appreciate you as a teacher. If you need to widen your circle, do not hesitate to contact me.

Kind regards,

Petite Loulou

Coming up next…

Book 3 – An Ever-Evolving Neighbouring Web

Preview:

We have a neighbour and friend who is the most ardent defender and supporter of our National Health Service. Almost every single day, the news reports how the NHS is in crisis and in need of restructuring. This is enough to send our neighbour-friend railing and complaining for hours…

He and Peter, his next-door neighbour, always end up in big arguments because the latter is a hypochondriac and spends more time at his GP than at home, that is according to Steve. Last year alone, Peter consulted his GP, was rushed to A&E, and was referred to specialists a total of fifty-seven times…

All of us children look forward to them arguing with each other about the NHS. And they do, without fail, at every one of our gatherings.

At our last get-together, Peter tried to avoid Steve like the plague. While we were busy playing in the garden, from time to time we would glance in their direction, or one of us, like a spy, would go near them when we sensed that World War III might break out.

We almost missed the beginning of the invasion. Lucky for us, Luke went on spying at the right time and immediately blew the whistle to signal the cold war had intensified, and a military conflict was imminent. From what we could observe, Steve had been wanting to engage on the subject for a good while. He would occasionally veer northwest toward Peter and ask him if everything was under control, to which an irritated Peter would answer an emphatic "yes."

In less than a couple of hours into our social gathering, Steve overheard Peter telling Harriett he was a very sick man and didn't think he would see the New Year. That was the moment Steve had been waiting for.

"Harriett don't listen to a word he says. He has been singing the same tune for the last twenty-five years, probably since he was born," Steve interjected.

The first missile had been launched and had hit the intended target. World War III had broken out, and all of us were anxious to follow its development. We positioned ourselves so as not to raise suspicion from either side. We had no intention of being allies or opponents in this conflict. We were determined to be only interested observers...

Available in June 2024

Check out **My Family, Kitten, & *Me*** series on Facebook, Twitter and Instagram for updates.

Printed in Great Britain
by Amazon

39025460R00066